A Guide to the Hidden Byways of London's Past

The Mews of London

Barbara Rosen & Wolfgang Zuckermann
Photographs by Christopher Wormald

Webb&Bower
EXETER, ENGLAND

Frontispiece : Kynance Mews at night.

First published in Great Britain 1982 by
Webb & Bower (Publishers) Limited
9 Colleton Crescent, Exeter, Devon EX2 4BY

Designed by Paul Watkins

Copyright © Webb & Bower (Publishers) Limited 1982

British Library Cataloguing in Publication Data
Rosen, Barbara
  The mews of London.
  1. London—History
  I. Title   II. Zuckermann, Wolfgang
  942.1   DA689.M/

  ISBN 0-906671-50-7

Typeset in Great Britain by August Filmsetting Limited,
Warrington, Cheshire

Printed and bound in Great Britain by
Hazell Watson and Viney Limited,
Aylesbury, Buckinghamshire

Contents

Introduction

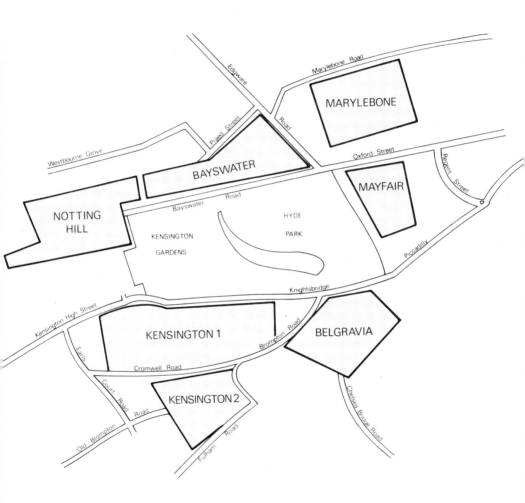

Map of the mews areas discussed in this book.

'If you wish to have a just notion of the magnitude of this city, you must not be satisfied with seeing its great streets and squares, but must survey the innumerable little lanes and courts. It is not in the showy evolutions of buildings, but in the multiplicity of human habitations which are crowded together, that the wonderful immensity of London consists.'

Samuel Johnson

NOTWITHSTANDING Dr Johnson, London's historians as well as tourists have unaccountably neglected this city's many hundred mews. In the immense literature about London there are few references to mews, and one looks in vain for a book about them.

Although overlooked by most outsiders, the mews are highly prized by their inhabitants and are much sought after by people seeking a quiet, central place to live and by estate agents who are always ready to extol their virtues. To the city dweller and city walker, the intricate network of these former stable blocks offers a respite from the tensions of city life. Their quiet, hidden and individual character almost always elicits a small shock of surprise and wonder.

This book traces the origin and development of the stable blocks, discusses their significance in present-day London, and takes the reader on a number of walks through the maze of central London mews. In selecting the mews for these walks, we have firstly considered their proximity to each other and central London, to make them easy walks. We have, secondly, looked for representative examples of mews architecture, from the grandiosely arched entrances and elegant houses of Kensington and Belgravia to the unadorned lanes of less fashionable districts, where the character of the original cottages can be observed more easily. For those unable to take the walks, we have provided photographs, descriptions and historical information to explain the individual mews.

The reader must remember that London, like all cities, changes from day to day and that some of the descriptions contained in this book may be out of date very soon. For example, we were distressed to discover, on passing the entrance to our Bayswater Walk recently, that the gate to Connaught Place was locked, due to impending development. On the other hand, we had a pleasanter surprise in Archery Close, where the cobbles miraculously reappeared after the modern paving was stripped away.

The charge is sometimes made that guide books destroy the hidden aspects of the objects they examine by the public scrutiny they give them; unlike Mark Antony they come to praise and end by burying. We express the hope that those readers of this book who are stimulated to explore the mews will do so with discretion, and will tread gently without disturbing the private character of these streets. We hope, too, that the public's increased awareness of this rich heritage will help stem the tide of development and planning which is making its destructive way across London.

The Mews
in London's
History

'THE MEWS of London,' wrote Henry Mayhew in 1851, 'constitute a world of their own. They are tenanted by one class—coachmen and grooms, with their wives and families—men who are devoted to one pursuit, the care of horses and carriages; who live and associate one among another; whose talk is of horses (with something about masters and mistresses) as if to ride or to drive were the great ends of human existence.'

Today, well over a hundred years later, the mews still constitute 'a world of their own'. Although the horses are gone, a vast maze of former stable blocks, rich in history and architectural oddities, remains. There are over six hundred of them left in modern London, most of them having certain features in common. They are cobbled; they are narrow, having no pedestrian footpath on either side; they are lined with small cottages, mostly Victorian two-storey houses; they were almost all former stables, and many still have their original stable doors and coach-house hardware; many are from three to nine feet lower than surrounding streets; and many are well hidden from the glance of the casual passer-by, and are entered through arches or discreet gateways, often set unobtrusively into a building façade. Though mews are to be found occasionally in other cities, their substantial number here makes them one of the factors which distinguish London from other great cities of the world.

The term 'mews' appears to come from the Royal Mews at Charing Cross, which was built on the site where the king's hawks were formerly 'mewed'. This meant that the birds were kept in a cage or mew at moulting time, the time they shed or changed their feathers. (The word derives from the French *muer*, to moult, which in turn comes from the Latin *mutare*, to change.) The Royal Mews was turned into a stable for horses in the sixteenth century during the reign of Henry VIII, and its new meaning of 'a set of stabling grouped around a yard or alley' was certainly known in the seventeenth century. Thus a mews called 'Blue Mews' appears in the rate book of St Martin's parish, Westminster, in 1659, and Rupert Mews, Soho, follows this into the Westminster Rate Book in 1677.

Mackay's map of 1723 shows the layout of some mews, and Roque's *Survey* of 1746 lists twenty-nine 'mewse' in its alphabetical index of London streets. (We shall encounter a number of these early mews in our Mayfair chapter.) From then on mews appeared with increasing frequency, ever keeping pace with London's expansion westward. But in order to discuss the origin of the mews, we must digress a little to describe briefly how London itself expanded through the development of its great estates.

Much of the land now occupied by London's West End was granted to followers of William the Conqueror after the Norman Conquest. (One such follower was Aubrey de Vere, whose name survives in the unusual mews we shall visit later.) These Normans in turn granted much of the land to religious institutions such as the Abbey of Westminster, some of whose estates, as we shall see in Bayswater, are still in the hands of the Bishop of London. But with the dissolution of the monasteries, vast

Previous page : Carriages parked in Woburn Mews; demolished in 1909.

holdings passed to Henry VIII, who sold, leased or gave away smaller parcels to his loyal courtiers.

Under Elizabeth I London thrived as a great commercial centre and there was much indiscriminate building, resulting in overcrowding and insanitary conditions. This phase of London's development ended with the Great Plague of 1665 and the Great Fire of the following year. The stage was now set for a general move westward and in the space of forty years St James's, Soho, Lincoln's Inn and parts of Bloomsbury rose from the green fields outside the walls of the ancient city. While a scattering of mews appeared in these new developments, these were mews in the dictionary sense of a set of stabling grouped around a yard or alley. The mews as a significant architectural entity made its appearance only after London's growth took an entirely new direction. This was the careful and conscious planning of the large estates, whose owners not only were in the fortunate position of having been able to hold on to their land through the Dissolution and the whims of Henry VIII, but of possessing land which lay exactly in the path of London's westward expansion.

The town planning which took place on the great estates introduced a number of unusual elements into the growth of London. Most cities had either grown haphazardly, or were planned on a grand scale (as were Rome and Paris), where the planning was executed by a central governmental authority. The concept of city planning as we know it (and fear it) today, did not exist. The great landlords of London were in the unique position of owning areas large enough to allow planning on a substantial scale, without being restricted either by lack of money or an interfering government. Even the richest landlords, however, might have run out of money for such ambitious projects, if they had not hit upon a system of leaseholds, in which they disposed of their land on long leases instead of selling their freehold interest or building on their property themselves.

The landlords could thus have their cake and eat it too. Most of the risks of building the houses and not recouping their investment, or of over-extending themselves in costly building speculation, were taken by the builders and sub-builders, who leased the land from the ground landlords. The estate owner and his descendants continued to collect the rent and own the land, regardless of the economic conditions prevailing at any particular time. At the end of the 89- or 99-year lease, the landlords' descendants were able to charge handsome premiums and raise the ground rents to many times their original figure. It must be remembered, however, that the ground landlords initially received very little profit from the building developments—ground rents were invariably low. These landlords, who were generally aristocrats, and dynastically conscious, were willing to take risks for the benefit of future generations, although they themselves may actually have taken a loss.

Frank Banfield, a social critic whose *The Great Landlords of London* (1888) was a vehement and impassioned plea against this leasehold system, imagines the following dialogue between an intelligent child of the future (our own time?) and his instructor: 'Who caused these houses to be built?' 'The Duke of Westminster.' 'Who paid for the building of these houses?' 'The Duke of Westminster's tenants.' 'Then they belong to the Duke of Westminster's tenants' children?' 'No, to the Duke of Westminster's children.' 'Was the Duke of Westminster very kind to the tenants?' 'He made them beautify his building land out of their own pockets, and took credit for that; charged them a heavy ground rent, and at the end of ninety-nine years they were to submit to reversion of the property to his descendants.'

In spite of this rather one-sided evaluation, the fact that this system of leasehold estate planning has produced so many spacious, green and elegant layouts, in many cases surviving unscathed to this day, demonstrates its success; a success which some may ascribe simply to the fortunate historical accident of these estates originating in the enlightened climate of the eighteenth and nineteenth centuries. Others might add that the planning of the estates, done primarily for profit, came to benefit the community as a whole and thus could be termed one of the 'acceptable' faces of capitalism. The leasehold system, which, according to Banfield, was the product of the 'calamitous' combination of organized interests and old Acts of Parliament, is held by Professor Donald J. Olsen to be responsible for much of London's elegance.

Banfield rightly objected to the immense concentration of wealth in the hands of a few estate owners, and to a system which prevented many ordinary people from owning their houses. He disparaged the idea that the leasehold system helped London's development. 'That London could not have grown but for great ducal landowners is a statement monstrously absurd, and rebutted by the fact that the many populous centres of industry in the North of England will only have houses in freehold,' he wrote. But he seems not to have considered the more subtle architectural ramifications of a system which made London a more interesting and elegant place than these populous northern centres of industry.

Perhaps a more equitable system might have been a series of long leases, which would have at first benefited the builders and planners of the estates, but which would eventually have reverted to freeholds to benefit the tenants themselves. (Something like this did happen, in fact, on estates like the Holland and Ladbroke which got into financial difficulties and were forced to sell off many of the freeholds to their land.)

The first of the big estates to be developed belonged to the Russell family, whose ancestor John, the first Earl of Bedford, had been granted the Covent Garden area by Edward VI in 1552. In addition to Covent Garden, the Bedford Estate included parts of Bloomsbury (a large area around what is now Bedford Square) and Figs Mead, north of Euston Station, later known as Bedford New Town.

The 4th Earl began the development of Covent Garden by obtaining a royal licence to demolish the old buildings in 1631. Thinking of a way to beautify the town, he called on the Palladian architect Inigo Jones, whose uniform, arcaded terraces in the Covent Garden Piazza (demolished in the nineteenth century) were reminiscent of the Place des Vosges in Paris. Olsen considers that the 'regular, classical layout of the Piazza in Covent Garden set standards in town planning that were to dominate upper and middle class urban architecture in the British Isles for more than two centuries.' According to Olsen, the Earl and Inigo Jones had created the prototype of the London Square. The Covent Garden residents were so pleased with the new square, that some of them named their daughters 'Piazza'.

However that may be, this first experiment in town planning was not a complete success. The market later overran the square, and no other squares were built in Covent Garden; there were many mean, narrow alleys behind the wide streets, and fashionable residents began to abandon the area in the eighteenth century. The Earl also granted some of the plots in perpetuity, making their owners practically freeholders. The descendants of these owners, not subject to the control of the estate, would later squeeze as many as half a dozen houses into a single plot.*

By the time the area around Bedford Square was developed in the latter part of the eighteenth century, the planning, according to Olsen, was 'of a more sophisticated variety, surpassed nowhere else in London'. For our purposes the Bedford Estate, apart from being the first planning unit on which later estates modelled themselves, is less interesting than some of these later estates. For a variety of reasons, many of the Bedford mews were pulled down at the end of the nineteenth century. Some had turned into slums, some gave way to gardens for the front houses, and many were gobbled up by institutions like London University. Perhaps the Bedfords were a little unlucky in the location of their estates; they were too far from the centres of fashionable London to hold people of means and their attendant staffs and carriages for any length of time. Much of the area degenerated into genteel boarding houses, and it became a mark of high breeding to pretend not to know where Bloomsbury was. Someone inquired in the House of Commons: 'But where is Russell Square?'

More important for us is the Grosvenor Estate, the largest in London, which has always appealed to the people of fashion (no one ever asked, 'but where is Grosvenor Square?') and thus has a high density of mews. The estate, including 'The Hundred Acres' in Mayfair, and parts of Belgravia and Pimlico, made the Grosvenors 'perhaps the wealthiest uncrowned house on earth' and led to their dukedom in 1874. It all started in 1677 when the guardians of twelve-year-old Mary Davies offered as a marriage portion to the young baronet Sir Thomas Grosvenor some five hundred acres of fields west of built-up London. Considering the tender age at which Mary Davies's fate was sealed, it is perhaps not surprising that in 1705 she was certified insane by a Commission of Lunacy especially appointed for the purpose.

*That the other estates avoided this error is shown by the fact that the ratio between freeholds and leaseholds in some London areas in 1887 was 1 : 7.

There was nothing remarkable in the Grosvenors' decision of 1720 to lay out 'The Hundred Acres' for building, because London was at that time in the grip of a building fever, well described by Daniel Defoe: 'I passed an amazing Scene of new Foundations, not of Houses only, but as I might say of new Cities, New Towns, new Squares, and fine Buildings, the like of which no City, no Town, nay, no Place in the World can shew; nor is it possible to judge where or when, they will make an end or stop of Building . . .' Observing the movement westward, the author of *Robinson Crusoe* continues: 'The City does not increase, but only the Situation of it is going to be removed, and the Inhabitants are quitting the old Noble

Streets and Squares where they used to live, and are removing into the Fields for fear of Infection; so that, as the People are run away into the Country, the Houses seem to be running away too.'

Roque's map of Grosvenor Square area in 1746 shows a good many mews, among them Reeve's, Adam's, Grosvenor, Shepherd's, Wood's and Brook's Mews. The *Survey of London* points out that in leases of plots which had their principal frontages on major streets (such as Brook Street or Grosvenor Square) and long return frontages to secondary streets, a condition was often inserted which allowed the building of stables only if no entrance led from even the secondary street to the stables. Access had

A View of Grosvenor Square (1753).

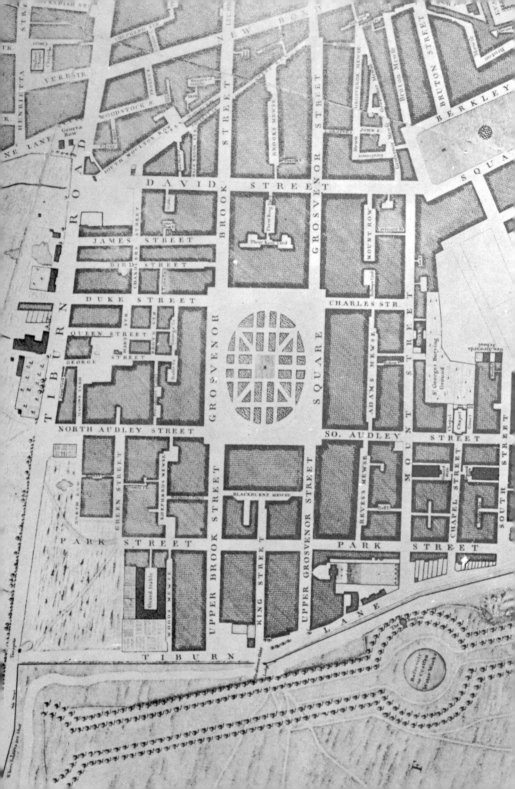

to be obtained from the mews at the rear. These mews were a kind of third-class street, running between two major streets, and being as self-contained as the planners could make them. The first-class citizens in the front houses did not wish to know of their existence, except when their horses and carriages were called for.

Olsen tells us that the eighteenth-century estates 'distinguished . . . carefully and efficiently . . . between streets of first, second, and third-rate houses; they permitted shops only in the narrower back streets, and prohibited offensive trades entirely. Yet all provided for several classes of society. Even Mayfair had its mean streets and narrow courts as well as a variety of services—from markets to mews—to benefit residents of the great houses in the principal streets and squares. Each estate was a varied, balanced community which excluded only the very poor, and industrial nuisances, on principle. Segregation, social and functional, took place between street and street, not between estate and estate.'

In this fashion evolved the architectural entity of the mews block, perfected by the same Grosvenor Estate many years later in Belgravia, when the mews were discreetly screened by arches cunningly set into principal street façades, at one stroke enhancing the front streets and hiding the mews.

Left: Roque's map of the Grosvenor Square area (1746).
Above: Hollywood Mews, which has its entrance set into a street façade.   17

It can be assumed that the mews in this form could only develop because the estates had large areas for town layouts at their disposal. Individual plot owners would probably have squeezed the stable buildings around a yard or into a four-storey building with ramps, and these types of stables were indeed found in areas outside the great estates. The *Survey* points out that the provision and location of the mews must have occupied much of the developers' thoughts, and goes on to wonder why no record of this has been found. The answer may well be that anything in connection with the mews was not deemed worthy of recording or even mentioning, a silence which continues in print to this day.

Although we have described only the Bedford and Grosvenor estates, a similar pattern of planning and building on long leaseholds was followed by the many other estates of London. We will encounter some of these like the Holland, Ladbroke, Bishop of London (Hyde Park), Smith's Charity, Portman, Pembridge and Crown estates on our various mews walks, but there were of course countless others. In most of them the ground landlord or estate owner did not do the actual building, although he had much to do with the planning; and not infrequently he was called upon to bail out the actual builder or sub-builders, who took much more of a risk.

Who were these speculative builders who, in spite of Nash's remark to the House of Commons that 'speculative building would be the death of English architecture', were in a large measure responsible for London's westward expansion? Olsen quotes John W. Papworth, who writes about that 'anomalous being': he 'need not be a builder, or a tradesman in any branch of building: indeed, the persons whom I have known succeed best, were a sailor . . . a chandler's shopkeeper . . . and a footman.' In other words, anyone with enough cash to invest and a dream of amassing a fortune. It is instructive to compare the splendid outcome of the collaboration between the estate owners and these amateur or would-be architects with the (anything but splendid) product of today's professional architects. To be fair, we should add that eminent architects and builders like Cockerell, Freake, Aldin, Allason and many others whom we shall encounter later, also greatly contributed to design and speculative building. But it is nonetheless true that the design of speculative housing lay with the builders, whose views on architecture remained traditional. *The Builder* observed in 1858 that 'what is really the architectural talent of the day has nothing to do with what becomes the character of London architecture'. The speculative builder decided according to his taste what style to build, based on his judgement of what would sell.

Olsen considers that 'perhaps the fundamental aim of all planning was to attract to the estate tenants of fashion or at least respectability. No landlord would feel the same pride in an estate of working-class tenements as in one whose residents stood higher on the social ladder.' This of course always meant much space devoted to mews. The *Survey of London* estimates the overall ratio of mews units to houses in the Grosvenor

Western London in 1806.

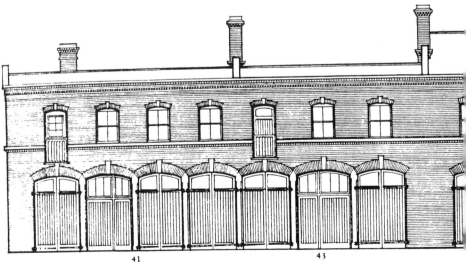

41   43

STRIP ELEVATION

Shop-keepers in Montagu
Mews, which was demolished
in 1898/99.

Mews block, Jay Mews.

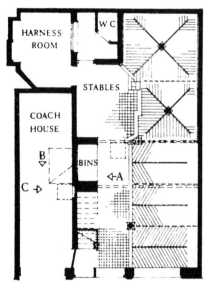

WC

HARNESS
ROOM

STABLES

COACH
HOUSE

B

BINS

C

←A

GROUND FLOOR

FEET
METRES

10   0   10

3   0   3

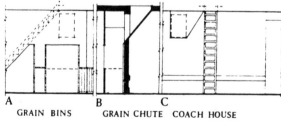

A
GRAIN BINS

B
GRAIN CHUTE

C
COACH HOUSE

45

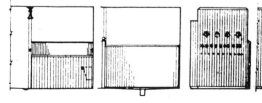

STALL

LOOSE BOX

HARNESS ROOM

Estate at about 1:1.4. In the 'best' residential parts there were probably as many stables as houses.

The *Survey* discusses the number of domestic servants in Grosvenor Square, and cites the 1841 census which revealed that more than three-quarters of all the Square's residents consisted of domestic servants. This census did not distinguish between domestic servants and coachmen, but if we consider that many others besides coachmen lived in the mews, we must begin to wonder how they all fitted into these cramped quarters.

For example, in Grosvenor Mews, a short distance away from the Square, the *Survey* mentions victuallers, chandlers, builders, servants and a chimney-sweep among the inhabitants, in addition to wheelwrights, farriers, stable-keepers and coachmen. Although some mews houses were impressively grand, like the one in Sackville Street cited by Byng Giraud, which could contain two riding horses and two carriage horses in addition to two 'slaves' for night work and three leaders for a victoria (plus all the carriages that went with these horses), most of them were much more modest in size. Every inch of space was needed on the ground floor for the coach-house, stalls or loose box, harness room, grain bins, and WC, not to speak of stairs to the upper quarter, if the coachmen and their families were to be left with liveable space upstairs. Examining the 1871 census results for an area of Kensington, the *Survey* found that 114 of the 120 coachmen in the sample were married, and many had children, grooms and other servants living with them as well.

The problem of people, horses and coaches in the mews houses was made much more difficult by the lack of ventilation caused by the almost total absence of rear or side windows. Residents of the elegant front houses with their private gardens did not wish to be overlooked by the mews dwellers, and the mews builders consequently made no provision for rear windows. Since the houses were almost always in a row and of uniform height, there was no space for side windows either. Byng Giraud, an architect whose book *Stable Building and Stable Fitting* (1891) lays down the rules for proper stables, bemoans the fact that since space is more valuable in town than in the country, 'where a stable is built in a mews, the length is at right angles, and not parallel as it should be, to the frontage), leading to a lack of light and ventilation. He stipulates the minimum frontage which should be allowed for a coach-house and stable as 25 feet, but complains that the 'coach-house in a mews, however, is often only 8'6'' or 9' in width, and if two carriages are kept, they are put one behind the other'. He is also dissatisfied with the position of the loose box at the back, as that part of the stable is often 'dark and difficult to ventilate and unsuited to its purpose'.

The necessity of proper ventilation becomes clear when we consider the sanitary conditions in the mews. The *Survey* points out that the water closets were usually ventilated from the staircase, and urinals *à la mode française* were used by the army of outdoor servants who worked there. A constant supply of water was not provided even in Mayfair until the

1890s. This made it hard to comply with Giraud's advice about cobbles, which he considered 'unsanitary for stables, and requiring, owing to their irregular character, a great deal of flushing in yards and passages'.

The problem was not helped by the enormous quantities of dung for which the Grosvenor Estate leases instructed the tenants to 'sink a place . . . in the said street . . . for the holding and keeping of such Dung and . . . cover the same over in a Safe manner'. The fact that they were not always covered over 'in a safe manner' was suggested in Dickens's description in *Little Dorrit* of the 'boudoir commanding the dunghills in the Mews'. It is small wonder that John Hollingshead in his *Ragged London in 1861* describes the mews of St Marylebone as 'hell holes . . . heaped with rubbish . . . with unendurable stench'.

The problem was made worse by the grooms' habit of stacking up the manure until they had enough of it to sell to a market gardener for a few shillings. A writer in the *Medical Times* complained that '. . . of this manure there are always (at moderate computation) remaining daily in the mews and stable yards of the metropolis, at least 2,000 cart-loads'. No wonder one of the early mews was called Dunghill Mews!

Dr Hillier, the medical officer for St Pancras, gave this description to a deputation from the sanitary boards of St Pancras and St George: 'The staircases are narrow and dark; the rooms are small and low; under the stairs is a damp, dirty, and offensive privy . . . The water tank is close to the privy and its contents are . . . charged with effluvia from it. There is no back ventilation . . . Each room is occupied by a family. The passages and rooms are out of repair and very dirty.'

Dr Hillier published an article in 1859 entitled 'On the Mortality in

Hays Mews, probably the last urinal *à la mode française* in a London mews.   23

the Mews' in which he cited the death rate in the three years from 1856–8 for the general population of St Pancras as 23 per thousand, but that of the mews as 26.45 per thousand. The specific diseases listed as exceeding the general death rate included pulmonary affections, measles and scarlatina; twice as many infants died in the mews from 'nervous' diseases including teething and convulsions as in the rest of the parish; and the general death rate for the under-fives was considerably higher in the mews, suggesting that this was no place to bring up children.

Yet the healthier children might have derived a great deal of pleasure and excitement from their life in the mews. Ernest Shepard, the illustrator of *Winnie the Pooh*, recalls the nearby mews of his childhood visits as 'a most interesting place with plenty going on—horses being groomed and harnessed, carriages washed or polished, the grooms hissing and whistling at their work. Strings of washing hung from the upper windows, whence the womenfolk leaned out and chatted to the men below.' Michael Faraday grew up in Jacob's Well Mews, and the greater part of the future scientist's time must have been spent among the horse litter in this by-lane.

Although Henry Mayhew, whom we quoted earlier, appears to have overlooked the fact that many tradesmen outside the horse-world lived and worked in the mews, the horse-related trades always accounted for the principal business of every mews. To Mayhew's coachmen and grooms, with their wives and families, Frank Huggett adds a number of characters who 'seem to congregate around horses like flies: commission agents, touts, copers, dealers, corn chandlers, bookmakers, strappers, and casual labourers'.

Mayhew describes a conversation with an old, consumptive man living in one room above some stables in Tottenham Mews. He occupied himself by polishing harness for a few pence; his room contained barely any furniture save for his few treasures: a lithograph of a horse, a Hogarth etching, and a stuffed bird. His wife was equally old and helpless and his thirty-seven-year-old son, who was lame, purblind and of subnormal intelligence, made a few pence a week as a crossing sweeper.

Huggett, in *Carriages at Eight* gives the following description of a typical day in the mews:

Work started in the mews . . . at 5 a.m. in the summer and 6 a.m. in the winter, so that the head coachman, after having a late breakfast at 10 a.m., could report at the big house to receive the orders of the day, confident in the knowledge that he could turn out well-groomed horses and immaculate carriages, without a speck of dirt inside or outside, within twenty minutes of his masters' or mistress' command. Before he had his breakfast the stables had to be cleaned, the horses had to be groomed and fed, and the carriages and harnesses had to be polished. The coachman usually groomed the carriage horses, while the groom looked after the riding horses. Each horse was thoroughly cleaned from the tip of its ears to the soles of its feet to free its skin of all accumulated scurf, dirt, and sweat. The ears were gently massaged for a few minutes until they were warm and then wiped out with a damp sponge; the hooves were washed and the dirt picked out before they were anointed in Victorian times with a mixture of oil and lamp black

Opposite, above : Charlotte Mews (1909).
Opposite below : The east side of Upper Montagu Mews (1915).

in the mistaken belief that it would increase the growth of the horn. The whole process took about one-and-a-half hours and at the end of it the master expected the coat to be so clean that it would not 'soil a cambric handkerchief'. The carriages were thoroughly cleaned, the body with a soft sponge or a cloth mop, the wheels with a spoke brush, and the leather braces with an oily rag. Servants were also expected to check each carriage for safety, though they were often negligent in this respect, which sometimes had disastrous consequences for their employers.

Huggett points out that if a carriage was to be used only three times a day, it was necessary to employ two coachmen and two grooms. Most of the high-class coachmen, according to Huggett, modelled themselves on the pattern of the Royal Mews, where an almost military discipline was maintained. The head coachmen had to be between thirty and forty years of age. Before that they were too 'lacking in authority'; after forty they were too 'dim-sighted, lazy, or drunk'. Grooms could be dismissed for any small negligence.

London coachmen were proud of their equipages and had their own recipes for horses' ailments or liquid blacking. Huggett cites the case of a titled lady's coachman, who gave two of her most valuable horses his patent remedy for influenza, which successfully killed off the horses within forty-eight hours! The head coachmen or their wives spent their time brewing polishes in cauldrons kept bubbling in some corner of the mews. One recipe that was cited by Huggett for liquid blacking contained mutton suet, purified beeswax, lamp black, turpentine, sugar candy and soft soap.

'Gentlemen,' wrote Sir George Stephen, 'are always more fidgety and precise on matters that relate to their pleasures, than on other points of domestic economy. If the ... stables ... are not in order, more dissatisfaction is expressed than if the dinner is spoilt.' The mistresses could be even more inconsiderate than the masters. Huggett writes of some ladies making a habit of overloading their carriage with too many large parcels and fat friends, which brought the master's wrath down on the coachman for putting the strain on the horse. Society people often had a greater concern for their horses than for their stable staff. According to Huggett, coachmen had to wait around for hours in the rain, sleet or snow while their employers enjoyed themselves in a warm dining room or theatre. The best horses, however, were spared these night ordeals; no-one who valued a good horse would dream of allowing him to stand exposed to chilly blasts at the opera.

The upper classes, which thus put a higher value on their horses than their grooms, did no more than act in accordance with the mores and dictates of the prevailing fashion. Disraeli, in his novel *Sybil*, sums up early nineteenth-century attitudes in describing the two nations of rich and poor into which the country was divided: '... between whom there is no intercourse and no sympathy, who are as ignorant of each others' habits, thoughts and feelings, as if they were dwellers in different zones or inhabitants of different planets: who are formed by a different breeding, are fed by a different food, are ordered by different manners, and are not governed by the same laws.'

Today, when we look with increasing nostalgia upon the days of the horse, it is instructive to be reminded that they were far from quiet and peaceful. Thomas Carlyle considered London 'the noisiest Babylon that ever raged and fumed on the face of the planet'. The architect H. B. Creswell, writing in the *Architectural Review* of December 1958, reminisced about his childhood days in the early 1890s:

> The whole of London's crowded wheeled traffic—which in parts of the City was at times dense beyond movement—was dependent on the horse: lorry, wagon, bus, hansom and 'growler', and coaches and carriages and private vehicles of all kinds . . . Meridith refers to the 'anticipatory stench of its cab-stands' on railway approach to London; but the characteristic aroma—for the nose recognized London with gay excitement—was of stables . . . whose middens kept the cast-iron filigree gas chandeliers that glorified the reception rooms of middle class homes . . . encrusted with dead flies and, in late summer, veiled with jiving clouds of them. A more assertive 'mark of ze 'orse' was the mud that, despite the activities of a numerous corps of red-jacketed boys who dodged among wheels and hooves with pan and brush in service to iron bins at the pavement edge . . . flooded the street with churnings of 'pea soup' that at times collected in pools over-brimming the kerbs, and . . . covered the road-surface as with axle grease or bran laden dust to the distraction of the wayfarer. In the first case, the swift-moving hansom or gig would fling sheets of such soup—where not intercepted by trousers or skirts—completely across the pavement, so that the frontages of the Strand, throughout its length had an eighteen-inch plinth of mud-parge thus imposed upon it. The pea-soup condition was met by wheeled 'mud carts' each attended by two ladlers clothed as for Icelandic seas in thigh boots, oilskins, collared to the chin, and sou'westers sealing the back of the neck. Splash Ho! The foot passenger now gets the mud in his eye! . . . Hence arose London's shoe-blacks, registered and red-coated, at the kerbside doing a mighty job with blacking and spittle for 2d; and hence also London's crossing-sweeper of the fashionable quarters. And after the mud the noise, which, again endowed by the horse, surged like a mighty heart-beat in the central districts of London's life. It was a thing beyond all imaginings . . . the hammering of a multitude of iron-shod hairy heels upon [the streets], the deafening, side-drum tattoo of tyred wheels jarring . . . like sticks dragging along a fence; the creaking and groaning and chirping and rattling of vehicles, light and heavy, thus maltreated; the jangling of chain harnesses and the clanging or jingling or every other conceivable thing else, augmented by the shrieking and bellowings called for from those of God's creatures who desired to impart information or proffer a request vocally—raised a din that, as has been said, is beyond conception. It was not any such paltry thing as noise. It was an immensity of sound . . .

The days of 'ze 'orse' so graphically described above ended with the introduction of the motor-car. The *Survey* reports that in Queen's Gate Mews a 'motor car house' was built for a Captain G. D. Sampson of Hyde Park Gate in 1898. Estate agents were beginning to think that too many stables had been built for the demand. Already in 1888 the occupants of Queen's Gate refused to build stables behind their houses, and the estate surveyors agreed that elsewhere houses were selling without them.

For a long time London had had good public transport. The omnibus had been introduced to London as early as 1829 and provided a general alternative to the private carriage, making it feasible for the gentleman of limited means to reside farther than walking distance from his place of business. In 1846 these services were good enough to lead to Thackeray's delighted exclamation (after his move to Kensington): 'and omnibuses every two minutes . . . what can mortal man want more?' (Anyone who has ever waited for a bus in modern London will be in a position to appreciate Thackeray's delight.)

Already by the 1840s, Olsen writes, 'the rich were not content to have the poor decently screened off in a near-by mews or court, but wished to escape from their proximity entirely.' By the 'fifties the suburban train would extend still further the possibilities of residence. The omnibus and the train permitted middle-class neighbourhoods to dispense with the mews. As early as 1849, Peter Cunningham's *Handbook of London* points out, 'few residents on the [Bedford] estate now kept their carriages; consequently the mews, including those which then occupied a quarter of the university site, gradually became livery stables, probably with many more occupants, equine and human, than before.'

The mews in fashionable districts, unlike those of middle-class neighbourhoods, remained more or less as they were. The upper classes, many of whom refused to travel by public transport, continued to rely on their private carriages and on their grooms. When the motor-car came in, these

people took to it as a private and efficient means of getting around London, and the original purpose for which the mews were built was quickly abandoned.

The *Survey* regrets that it has not been possible to 'trace chronologically the conversion of stables to garages. Nor is evidence forthcoming to plot the change overhead of residential mews-accommodation from the home of servants to the "amusing" address of the smart and then to the ordinary home of small fairly well-to-do families.' However, a period of some years elapsed between the abandonment of horses and the 'amusing' mews addresses referred to above. In the meantime, a number of mews, as they had for a long time threatened to, descended into conditions of poverty.

The two sets of maps, one dated 1889 and the other 1900, in Charles Booth's *Life and Labour of the People in London* give some indication of this process. Booth's maps employed various colours to indicate well-being or poverty. In the 1889 map of the Bedford Estate there are only two small blue (really poor) patches. The little mews houses are all coloured pink, meaning that their inhabitants enjoyed 'working-class comfort'. The 1900 map shows some deterioration; the mews east of Upper Bedford Place and Keppel Mews have sunk into the blue which denotes poverty. The former stables now became the dwellings of the many people living and working in London's better neighbourhoods who could not afford to live anywhere else.

The great estates tried their best to improve this situation. The *Survey* notes the 'widespread rebuilding of coach-houses and stables' in Mayfair and the rehousing of their former occupants. According to the *Survey*, a lot of this improvement in the mews took place 'in the years immediately preceding the gradual eclipse of the horse by the motor-car. By 1910 tenants on the [Grosvenor] estate were said to have a general desire to get rid of horses.' The *Survey* cites as the first known example of a stable conversion into a dwelling house No 2 Aldford Street (then No 1 Streets Mews) in 1908. We must remember that the mews in Mayfair were 'equine palaces' compared with the average London mews house, and thus well suited for 'residents no longer able or willing to live in a great house in one of the fashionable streets'.

This signalled the advent of the 'bijou' mews house in Mayfair. The *Survey* speculates that motor-cars 'possibly' took up less space than horses; in fact, they must have taken up infinitely less space when one considers carriages, harness rooms, grain bins, hay and dung storage, etc. in addition to the horses themselves. In 1908 the Grosvenor Board agreed to the conversion of stables in Balfour Mews and Streets Mews which were letting badly, and five years later a storey was added to No 1 Balfour Mews. A speculator called Matheson reported 'great demand' for what he called 'bijou housing' and one post-war conversion was considered worthy of publication in *Country Life*. We shall see some of these elaborate conversions later, and they are interesting as a comment on the history of the mews, but they are far from typical of the rest of London. Most of Lon-

Keppel Mews in 1900, demolished in 1901.

don's mews houses were too small for the elegant conversions which would suit people of fashion, at least at that time. Later, with space becoming ever more expensive and scarce, the middle and upper classes were to flock to the mews in the same large numbers as the poorer working classes had done fifty years earlier.

In spite of some radical conversions, much of the intimate and original character of the mews remained. Byng Giraud had written in 1891 that 'Collinge's hinges are the best for coach-house and entrance gates and are made upon the principle of the ball-and-socket, the latter forming a receptacle for oil . . .' Collinge's patented hinges (the firm is still in business) were indeed in almost universal use in the mews, and are still very much in evidence today. Their presence on stable doors usually indicates that the doors are original. It is always regrettable when mews dwellers remove the original doors and replace them with modern overhead doors,

An original stable door replaced by a modern overhead garage door.

which are much harder to handle, take up space in the garage, and cannot be closed from the inside, apart from being out of character and unsightly.

The cobbles★ and arches which characterize so many mews are also still very much in evidence, and fortunately many mews dwellers have left the façades of their houses unchanged except for a coat of paint over the bricks. In some cases, especially when all the façades in a mews have been painted, this can brighten the general appearance, but it is equally pleasant to encounter the original brick fronts as in Palace Gardens and Linden Mews. We shall discuss the present state of the mews in our concluding chapter, but we may offer a brief prayer of thanks for the historical obscurity of the mews which seems to have been largely responsible for their preservation.

★Most of the mews are paved with square or rectangular granite blocks called setts. We have used the more colloquial term of cobbles, although strictly speaking cobbles are small and rounded. Nevertheless, Byng Giraud in his *Stable Building and Stable Fitting* (1891) refers to cobbles and observes that 'when carefully selected and laid by an expert, the boulders not being too small, the old cobble stones form a durable paving and give a good foothold to the horses'.

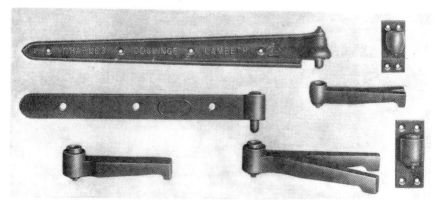

The Lambeth factory of Charles Collinge & Co Ltd, with examples of Collinge's hinges.   31

A stable ramp in one of the few large working stables left in London. This one, in the East End, belongs to the Whitbread Brewery.
Opposite: Wood's Mews, Mayfair (1969); a former 'equine palace'.

Bayswater

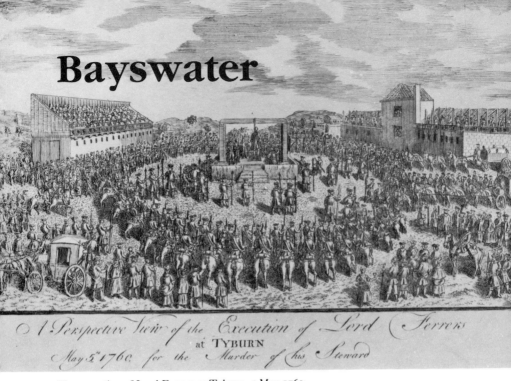

A Perspective View of the Execution of Lord Ferrers at TYBURN May 5 1760 for the Murder of his Steward

The execution of Lord Ferrers at Tyburn, 5 May 1760.

IN 1783, when the last execution took place at the Tyburn Gallows, London did not extend beyond what is now Marble Arch, and Paddington and Bayswater were isolated villages. Tyburn Tree, as the gallows was known, first stood at the junction of Edgware Road and Tyburn (Oxford) Street and was later moved to the site of Connaught Square in Tyburnia, providing a popular entertainment for the villagers and Londoners who gazed upon the demise of famous and infamous alike. Oliver Cromwell's disinterred body was hanged, beheaded and buried beneath the gallows, and the celebrated highwayman Jack Sheppard, described as dangerous but charming to women, must have aroused female sympathies at his execution.

As far back as the Middle Ages the Manor and Parish of Paddington formed part of the lands of the Abbey of St Peter's, Westminster. After the Dissolution the land came into the possession of the Bishops of London, who exercised control over it from then on, first under the administration of the Ecclesiastical Commissioners, later the Paddington Estate Trustees, and finally the Church Commissioners.

Tyburnia, then the open ground between Bayswater and Marble Arch where we start our walk, was described in Thackeray's *Catherine*: 'A hundred years ago [in 1739] Albion Street was a desert. The Square of Connaught was without its penultimate, and strictly speaking "naught". The Edgware Road was then a road, 'tis true; with tinkling wagons passing now and then, and fragrant walls of snowy hawthorne blossom. The ploughman whistled over Nutford Place; and down the green solitudes of Sovereign Street the merry milkmaid led the lowing kine.'

When the Grand Junction Canal Company received parliamentary permission to develop a canal basin at Paddington in 1795, London began expanding further westward. In the same year the Bishop of London obtained statutory powers to grant leases of land 'for the purpose of building upon' to fulfil a demand for residences near London. The Bishop endeavoured not only to emulate, but to surpass the examples of the earlier aristocratic estates in grandeur.

To this end the Bishop engaged the eminent architect Samuel Pepys Cockerell, designer of Mecklenburgh and Brunswick Squares. The copy of his plan for Tyburnia, dated 1824, shows a rather grand neoclassical design with Grand Junction Street (now Sussex Gardens) dividing the industrial canal basin area to the north from the residential district to the south, and connecting New (Marylebone) and Uxbridge (Bayswater) Roads. There was to be a large open space called the Polygon, which was in fact later filled up by Cockerell's successor, the pragmatic George Gutch, who revised Cockerell's street patterns, increased the number of houses, and built two squares in the Polygon. Curiously, the names of 'Junction' and 'Polygon' survive in mews, though the Church Commissioners managed to destroy Polygon Mews by the erection of large blocks of flats out of keeping with the character of Tyburnia. (Many modern maps of London still show Polygon Mews.)

Far enough from the City to be quietly residential, yet close enough to Mayfair, St James's and Westminster, Tyburnia in the early nineteenth century quickly established itself as a fashionable suburb, particularly for those affluent enough to own private carriages. With this wave of the well-to-do came their grooms, coachmen and horses, for whom the builders had provided many mews blocks. As we have already seen, ample mews space had to be provided in order to attract this class of people, and in Tyburnia and Bayswater we thus find some of the longest mews, like Bathurst, Hyde Park Gardens and Lancaster. Luckily, many of them have survived to this day, making this a fruitful area for mews exploration.

Though the mews were a necessity to attract the wealthy, we have already seen that polite society literally turned up its nose at them. In leases, rent books or directories they were often not considered important enough to be listed separately, being taken for granted as belonging to the front houses. Thus the Paddington Street Directory does not deign to mention Hyde Park Gardens Mews until 1910, and does not give any entries therein until 1923, and then ironically with 'Motor Cars for Hire'. The London Post Office Directory ignores this mews even then and only acknowledges its existence in 1930. Yet Hyde Park Gardens Mews was officially named in 1847, and there are leases dating from the early 1840s.

Though by the mid-1830s stucco was replacing brick-facing almost everywhere in Tyburnia, the unpretentious mews cottages continued with

A VIEW of the BASON of the GRAND JUNCTION CANAL at PADDINGTON

NAVIGATION

TRADE

A View of the FIRST BRIDGE and ACCOMMODATION BARGE of the GRAND JUNCTION CANAL at Paddington

their unadorned brick fronts. The leases were rather strict in what they did or did not allow people to do with their houses. In a standard lease form dated 4 May 1841 for a stable and coach-house in Hyde Park Gardens Mews, the tenant is warned that 'no erections should be set up in the yards or gardens or on any part of the premises . . . which might lessen the air obstruct the light or in any way interupt the view from the adjoining buildings or destroy the uniformity of the premises or which might cut or maim any of the principal timbers or walls of the buildings . . . and not to make any alterations in the plan and elevations of the said messuage or tenement coach-house and stable or in the cornices columns pilasters bases caps window sills mouldings rustics ballusters door cases windows or other architectural decorations . . . without license in writing of the said trustees.' A lease of 1842 for Conduit Mews added 'and shall not raise the said premises above their present height of the said Mews'.

Having originally issued this set of breathless and comma-less restrictions, the Trustees later proceeded (in the case of the Hyde Park Gardens Mews stable) to allow the tenant to 'take down the stables and rebuild same in brickwork, forming three stalls loose box harness rooms and coach-house on the ground floor and living rooms and bedrooms on the first floor and bedrooms and loft on the second floor'. (The licence to do this work was dated 8 November 1892.) The licence granted for No 7 Bathurst Mews in a lease originally dated 1842 was even more radical: to 'convert the stable consisting of coach-house, stable and two rooms into a single room by removing the roof, staircase, floors, partitions, stalls and coach-house. To brick up all openings in the external wall towards Bathurst Mews, to cover the existing stable and coach-house floor with concrete and form a new floor. To form a new roof with lantern light therein—to thicken the party walls where necessary—and to form a new fire place chimney breast and flue for the new room.' It seems from this that current conversions of mews cottages are often a good deal less radical than these earlier ones.

We must call your attention to another unusual feature of this area (later copied elsewhere) which Gordon Toplis, writing in *Country Life*, calls 'Back-to-Front Splendour'. This was Cockerell's idea of putting the entrances of some of the grand terraces facing the park behind rather than in front of their imposing façades, where the entrance presumably belonged. This gave him a chance to provide the principal rooms with a south-facing view over the park, but allow access from a quiet side street instead of the busy thoroughfare in front. Not inconsiderable was the advantage thus gained of having easy access to the carriages in the mews instead of manoeuvring them into the main road. We can see a good example of this in Connaught Place, adjacent to Connaught Mews, and Hyde Park Gardens, adjacent to the mews of that name.

In this walk, we shall move from east to west, following London's expansion in the same direction, and observing its imprint on the humble mews as well as on the more imposing buildings.

A souvenir of the Grand Junction Canal; it was sold to boatmen
who inserted the name of their boat in the centre space (1821).

BAYSWATER WALK

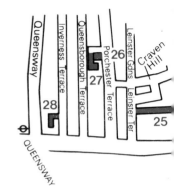

We start our walking tour at the north-west corner of Marble Arch and enter Connaught Place from Edgware Road through a black iron gate. No 7 was the residence of the eccentric Caroline, Princess of Wales (and later Queen), and it was hither that her daughter Princess Charlotte hurried one March day in 1814 to announce that she had broken off her engagement to Prince William of Orange. Presumably the back-to-front arrangement of the houses in Connaught Place made her clandestine visit less noticeable, though history records that she was eventually discovered and 'kicked and bounced but would not go'.

Today we are greeted by a noisy fan at the entrance to **Connaught Mews** which is the price these mews dwellers must presumably pay for being so close to busy Edgware Road. The view to the east is somewhat marred by the tall buildings dominating the horizon, a legacy of the modern 'Great Plague' which the developers inflicted on London in the mid-twentieth century. The original mews dwellers, however, had to contend with bones from the former gallows: 'In 1811, Dr Lewis [was] about to erect some houses in Connaught Place, and during the excavation a quantity of human bones was found. A good many of the bones, say a cartload, were taken away . . . and buried in a pit dug for the purpose in Connaught Mews.'

The original stable doors still seem to be in use in some of the cottages, suggesting a smooth transition from stables to garages. Connaught Mews already appears unnamed on a map of 1827, and received its name officially

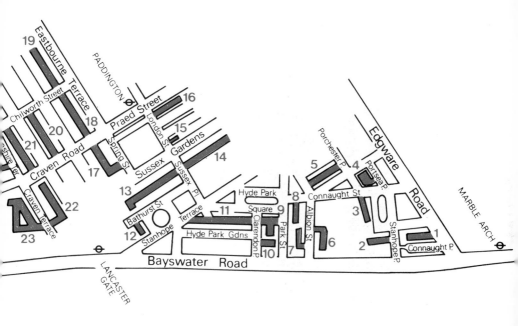

in 1847. It is interesting to contrast the rents of Connaught Place and Connaught Mews in 1819. The register of leases of the Paddington Estate for that year show that ground rents in Connaught Place varied from £40 to £80 per annum whereas rents in Connaught Mews averaged only £2 per annum.

Continuing via Connaught Place and Stanhope Place, we turn left into **Frederick Close**, until 1934 called Frederick Mews, after the wealthy Frederick family who acquired the manor of Paddington in 1741. The first house is interesting in that it follows the double-curved contour of the mews. The mews is enhanced by the stately trees in the private garden at its end. The substantial building on the north side has the dates 'founded 1816, rebuilt 1916' inscribed in its façade. Frederick Mews appears in the Post Office Directory as early as 1856, with No 1 being occupied by a livery stable and No 6b by a gas fitter.

Proceeding now via Connaught Square (where it is said that the Tyburn gallows stood on the site of No 49) and Connaught Street, we encounter **Archery Close**, somewhat spoiled by the modern paving hiding its former cobbles. The vine-covered cottage at its dead-end still recalls a stable, and many of the houses are painted in bright colours which may not be to everyone's taste, but lend them an individual touch. The west side presents a uniform façade with its handsome windows topped by gentle Victorian arches. The wavy roof-line of these buildings suggests the roof-tile projections so common in the eaves of south-eastern France.

Archery Close (1980). Note the roof-line and keystone details.
Below: Albion Mews (1959).

Archery Close was called Connaught Square Mews until 1936; the present name recalls a nearby archery ground used by the Royal Toxophilite Society until 1834.

Before continuing along Connaught Street you may wish to see what happened when the car replaced the horse, and the garage the stable, by looking at tucked-away **Portsea Mews** off Portsea Place, diagonally across from Archery Close. You may also wish to inspect the site of the former **Polygon Mews**, still marked on most maps as leading off Porchester Place, to decide whether an imaginative use was made of the former mews by the Hyde Park Estate developers.

Now turn left from Connaught Street into Albion Street and **Albion Mews,** called Albion Mews East until 1938. The Post Office Directory of 1850 shows a livery stable, cow-keeper and boot-maker resident there. Nos 22 and 21 provide a nice start to this mews, but the real surprise comes when you turn the corner to find two rows of well-groomed cottages. Large overhanging trees give this mews a rural aspect and compensate for the large grey building in the background. We especially liked the interestingly shaped No 20.

Now proceed to **Albion Close** opposite, until 1938 called Albion Mews West. This is an interesting collection of houses, each different in its own way. No 7 is somewhat unusual for having a wooden façade trying to suggest Tudor arches. No 8, lying in the dead-end, happened to be for sale at the time of our visit. This is the kind of mews property in which one could pursue a civilized life-style, provided one had the small fortune the owners asked for it. Free is the faint but omnipresent hum of Bayswater Road traffic. No 10 consists of two houses knocked into one and stuccoed to suggest a Spanish villa, perhaps not entirely convincing, and contrasting with the original stable doors and hardware of No 11.

Turning left on Connaught Street, we encounter **Connaught Close,** which was known as Albion Mews North until 1938, under which name it appeared on George Oakley Lucas's Parish of Paddington map dated 1847. This mews has not been smartened up like some of the others and at first sight may appear somewhat shabby. The Eastern row resembles turn-of-century photographs of unimproved mews cottages and thus reveals more of what the mews were like than its more affluent neighbours.

Continuing around the left side of Hyde Park Square, we turn into Clarendon Place and **Clarendon Mews,** bestowing a quick glance on its three prongs, the centre one of which has one row of interest. This, too, first appears in Lucas's 1847 map. From here we proceed to **Clarendon Close,** a more unusual arrangement of larger houses, some with gardens, grouped around a central yard. This was called Chester Mews until 1938, and also first appeared on the 1847 map of Paddington. As we have already seen, mews cottages with rear gardens were highly unusual, as the gardens invariably belonged to the grander front-house tenants, who did not wish to share them with their coachmen or even be overlooked by rear windows from the stables.

We now cross Clarendon Place and enter **Hyde Park Gardens Mews** through an attractive brick arch, not neglecting a look at the elaborately carved door of No 9 Clarendon Place. This mews is a long, open street of mostly two-storey cottages, whose façades vary from Victorian to modern, with various stages in between. The absence of neighbouring tall buildings here makes one almost forget that this is in the centre of one of the world's largest cities. The many potted plants and uninterrupted cobbles give the feeling of Provence, and there are a number of interesting decorative details to look at. The mews appears on the 1847 map, but was neglected by the directories.

Leaving Hyde Park Gardens Mews via Stanhope Terrace at its end and proceeding around Sussex Square to Bathurst Street, we reach **Sussex Mews West**. In contrast to **Sussex Mews East** which was not one of our 'Mews Fit To Print', this one is full of surprises. Note the roof balustrades of Nos 4 and 5. The mews turns the corner twice, promising new vistas, which, however, are better left unexplored. Sussex Square, from which the Mews derives its name, was begun in 1843, the year Prince Augustus, Duke of Sussex, died.

We now cross Bathurst Street into another extensive mews, all the more authentic for the generous amounts of horse manure. **Bathurst Mews** is another long, open street of low cottages, inviting their inhabitants to sit outside in sunny weather. There is a complex of stables in its right-angle turn which belong to the Hyde Park Riding Club, a welcome relief from the common mews garages. The mews gets its name from the same Frederick family we encountered earlier, one of whom married Elizabeth Bathurst of Clarendon Park in Wiltshire (thus Clarendon Close we passed earlier). Some of the houses in Bathurst Mews were fairly substantial, being shown on the old leases as having a depth of 47ft 3in. Yet the yearly ground rent on leases issued in the 1840s averaged only £2 on 92-year leases, to be paid in three instalments of 13s 4d each. Bathurst Mews first appears in the Post Office Directory for 1845 with the following inhabitants: No 1, Ed Munn, Corn & Coal Merchant; No 2, Thos Durell, veterinary surgeon; No 5, Thos Odell, dairyman; No 17, King Henry Livery stables; and No 18, Wm Dear, Fly proprietor; a fairly typical collection of mews dwellers.

In a report prepared for the Church Commissioners in 1972 by their planning consultant Leslie Lane, CBE, we read on page 46: 'Bathurst Mews will need to be the subject of a special study being situated behind the new Sussex Square flats and houses now to be retained in Sussex Gardens. Many of the present mews cottages are wholly unsatisfactory and a new scheme will have to be devised for this area.' One looks in vain for these 'wholly unsatisfactory' cottages—if they were there, they are an illustration of the process which Jane Jacobs calls 'unslumming'. The report, whose aims have not yet been abandoned, envisages a pedestrian zone with shops and offices in Bathurst Mews.

Cross Sussex Place into **Radnor Mews** which was known as Devonport

Right : An unusual display outside 27/28 Conduit Mews.

Hyde Park Gardens Mews.

Sussex Mews West; note the roof balustrades.

Bathurst Mews, a long open street of low cottages.

Sunday afternoon at the entrance to Bathurst Mews.

Mews until 1937; when it was renamed (along with countless other mews to avoid postal confusion) the new name was taken from Radnor Place to which this mews leads but access to which is now blocked. Radnor Place (and Bouverie Place) were named soon after young Lady Catherine Pleydell-Bouverie died in childbirth at Paddington in 1804, worn down, according to contemporary gossip, by the neglect and ill-treatment of her husband, the third Earl of Radnor, who was 'very immoral' in respect of female connections. The original character of some of the cottages in this mews can still be seen.

Now follow Sussex Place leading into London Street, and glance into **Norfolk Square Mews** in passing. Turn into **London Mews** which is interesting for showing how people live and work in a hidden corner of this busy section. Cross London Street and walk down Conduit Place opposite, noting Conduit Passage which leads to No 37, the Bake House, situated behind a turquoise gate.

Crossing Spring Street we come to **Conduit Mews**, a spacious, airy and sunny mews with many fine cottages in its southern row. Your attention is immediately arrested by No 27/28 with its many signs, rhymes, pots and plant-filled lavatory bowls. This kind of display would undoubtedly not be tolerated by the neighbours in an elegant Regency terrace, but hidden away in a mews where each house has its own individual touch it is not entirely out of place. There are pineapple-shaped stone ornaments on the roof of No 18; and No 16, with its recently renovated façade, suggests a Dutch bell-shaped gable. Craven Road, to which this mews leads, was formerly called Conduit Street, being adjacent to the former Conduit Fields. The Thames had ceased to be used for water supplies by the thirteenth century and water had to be piped in conduits and channels from the springs of Bayswater, a system which was in use until 1840.

Crossing Craven Road into **Chilworth Mews**, we must regretfully note that only its attractive southern row is extant. The northern row, having sustained some war damage, made way for a car park behind a 1950s style office tower block, which *The Times* of 2 September, 1957, praised for providing a 'refreshing contrast' to the more familiar main line station across the road. The open spaces for grass, trees and sculpture announced by *The Times* are not much in evidence. Chilworth Mews appears in the 1847 Paddington map as Charles Mews, which was its name until 1912, and under that name first appeared in the Post Office Directory of 1850.

A similar shotgun marriage of Victorian mews cottages with 1950s office towers awaits us at **Eastbourne Mews**, but we turn left on Chilworth Street and glance into **Gloucester Mews** with its derelict arch (see the leaflet 'Who Owns This Arch' reproduced on page 135) and pleasant south-facing row of mixed cottages. We turn left into **Upbrook Mews**, an abbreviation of Upper Brook Mews, which appeared unnamed on the 1847 Paddington map. Upbrook Mews is a good example of the

Lancaster Mews (1906).   Lancaster Mews (1980).

low level of some of the mews in relation to their surrounding streets, lying a good 9ft below Craven Road. Roads tended to be built up on causeways above true ground level, so that basement level at the front of the house corresponded to garden level at the back. Thus the stable buildings were sometimes at the same level as the service quarters in the basement of the big houses, and there could even be direct communication between them. The Westbourne Brook, running beneath this mews, meanders all over (or under) London. It appears in the most unlikely places, as for example in a large pipe in Sloane Square Underground station.

Now cross Craven Road to **Brook Mews North**, mainly noteworthy for the White Hart pub at its right-angle turn. This mews was built in 1850 and it, too, is exactly above the Westbourne Brook, by that time already forced into underground sewers, close to the point where it flows into the Serpentine. The mews is full of working garages, perhaps representing a natural transition from the horse, but resulting in rather more traffic and pollution than is usually found in a mews. The paving adds another unwelcome modern touch, and though this is not perhaps a quaint environment for its residents, it, like many other mews of that type, makes an ideal street for small businesses.

Directly across we see The Mitre pub with its cut-glass windows and honky-tonk music, which denotes the entrance to **Lancaster Mews**. This is a long, roughly circular mews with many fine houses. Turn right, leaving the garages and offices behind, and note the decorative brick detail

along the roof-line of the southern row, as well as the arched doorways of Nos 33–35. The mews turns the corner and branches out straight and to the left, seeming to go on and on but leading us back into Craven Terrace, along which we continue to Devonshire Terrace and **Craven Hill Mews**. This derives its name from the first Earl of Craven, who courageously stayed in London during the Great Plague of 1665 while others fled. The land he contributed in St Martin's as a burial ground was later exchanged for three acres in Paddington known as the Pesthouse Estate. Craven Hill, Craven Hill Gardens, Craven Road, Craven Terrace and Craven Hill Mews were all on this site.

Craven Hill Mews appears on the 1847 Paddington map, and the Post Office Directory for 1856 shows Nos 1, 2 and 3 occupied by John Trigg, Livery Stables. (Directory entries would usually show only tradesmen independent of the front houses.) This mews is very peaceful, being well hidden yet very bright, a seeming oasis with birds singing and traffic noise very faint. Even though the mews buildings themselves are ranged only along the south side, some of them are unusually large and with gardens, the backs of the larger houses opposite do not detract from the character of the mews. There is a modern brick complex at the end with a round tower, projecting windows and terraces.

Turn back to Devonshire Terrace and right into Craven Hill leading to Leinster Terrace, where at the Leinster Arms you will find the entrance to **Leinster Mews**, dominated by the steeple of Christ Church. This is

Leinster Mews; the steeple of Christ Church can be seen in the background.

another sunny, quiet cul-de-sac, with many of its houses having had upper storeys added. There are a variety of vines and ivies covering the houses, getting more profuse as we proceed to the dead-end. This mews was called Cleveland Mews until 1925, when the Council decided to match it with Leinster Terrace, built in about 1850. In 1955, when the Church Commissioners found themselves short of money, they auctioned off the freeholds to Nos 1–28 Leinster Mews, thus setting the mews free after a hundred years of dependence on the estate.

Go back down Leinster Gardens and cross over into Craven Hill Gardens turning right into Porchester Terrace. Here we find the impressive arch which denotes the entrance to **Fulton Mews**, one of the few arches which has been upgraded along with the rest of the mews, as can be seen from our comparative photographs. The arch was built in about 1845 and the name of the mews approved in 1871. The front houses are rather grand additions to the mansions of Porchester Terrace, but further on the buildings become more mews-like in character. Note the quiet courtyard space of No 12. The mews ends in a T-junction which is interesting in both directions and has overhanging trees at both ends.

Fulton Mews arch before restoration (1957).   After restoration (1980).

We next turn left into Queensborough Passage leading to **Queensborough Mews**. Note the unpaved road, perhaps one of the few dirt roads left in London. The real treat comes at the end when you turn left into the blind alley where some secluded cottages are situated. The mews got its name from John Aldridge, MP for Queensborough, whose wife, Henrietta Busby, had earlier brought the land into the Aldridge family. Now leave by the Queensborough Studios iron gate and proceed, via Bayswater Road, to Inverness Terrace and the hidden entrance to **Fosbury Mews**.

This mews is entered through a gate marked private and should be looked at quietly. Here, only yards away from the Bayswater Road, grass grows between cobbles and houses are covered in creeper. This is yet another oasis in one of London's busiest quarters. Its unusual name was approved in 1868; Bebbington reports that Fosbury is a hamlet in Wiltshire but its connection with Bayswater is unknown. Here we must leave you, close to Queensway with its shops, restaurants and public transport. Our Notting Hill Walk, which is to follow, starts not very far from here.

Above : Queensborough Mews. *Right :* Fosbury Mews.

The Hippodrome Racecourse existed near Pembridge Road from 1836 to 1840.
It was here that some speculators may have made their first investments in the
Ladbroke Estate. The fence in the background was created to keep out
the 'rude and licentious populace of the neighbourhood'.

Notting Hill

THIS WALK will take us through the area of two great estates—Ladbroke and Holland. The Ladbroke Estate was probably acquired by Richard Ladbroke, Esquire (brother of Sir Robert Ladbroke, banker and Lord Mayor of London) in the mid-eighteenth century, and passed on to his descendant, James Weller Ladbroke. The Holland Estate was purchased in 1768 by Henry Fox, first Baron Holland, from William Edwardes, who was later created Baron Kensington. By a combination of bad luck and mismanagement, these two estates suffered misfortunes which some of the other great estates seem to have been spared.

For one thing, as Olsen points out, Notting Hill never rivalled Bayswater in fashion or pretentiousness. It never seems to have attracted a sufficient number of people of quality so necessary to the commercial success of an estate. For another, there were several financial crises, which brought building to an abrupt halt. For example, the *Building News* reported in 1857 that 'on the north-eastern portion of the ill-fated Notting-Hill estate, we regret to observe a very great number of buildings still standing in a deplorable condition . . .' Ladbroke Gardens in 1860 was a 'desert of dilapidated structures and decaying carcasses . . . few . . . would care to dwell in that dreary desolation—with the wind howling and vagrants prowling . . .'

There were many near or outright bankruptcies. John Henry Goddard, an architect, removed himself and his family to the Continent to escape his creditors; James Hall, a builder, went bankrupt in 1864; the Reverend Dr Samuel Walker lost most of the great fortune he had inherited, in the space of four years in building speculation; David Allan Ramsay, a nurseryman turned builder, went bankrupt in 1854. Even the heads of the large estates were affected by this rash of misfortune. Lord Holland was forced to mortgage Holland House in 1849, and when he died Lady Holland sold part of her estate for over £100,000, but was not able to settle any of her mortgages or even keep pace with her expenditure. The Hollands spent vast sums on their lavish residence and on grand parties at which they entertained all of fashionable London. Lady Holland was finally forced to dispose of the estate in 1874, though she continued to live at Holland House for the rest of her days. All these financial clouds did have their silver lining, as much of the open space around Holland House was preserved because building development had ceased. The Ladbroke Estate did not fare much better; after J. W. Ladbroke died in 1847, the estate passed to a distant cousin, Felix, who himself died in reduced circumstances after selling the greater part of his property.

All this meant that unlike, for example, the Duke of Westminster or the Bishop of London, who were able to hold on to most of their estates by a system of leaseholds, the Hollands and Ladbrokes lost most of theirs by being forced to sell their lands or grant freeholds. As the *Survey of London* notes, 'suburban building development seems, indeed, to have been as fickle in its rewards as gambling had been in earlier days on the

races at the Hippodrome [built in 1836 in the vicinity of the later Ladbroke Grove, and demolished four years later] where it may be that some speculators made their first investments on the Ladbroke estate before trying their luck and skill in the more durable field of brick and mortar'.

In spite of all this, some distinguished architects worked in this area. Thomas Allason prepared a plan for the layout of Notting Hill in 1823, and later lived there himself (in Linden Grove, later called Linden Gardens) until his death in 1852. In the 1850s Charles Blake and the ill-fated Dr Walker began the imaginative succession of terraces and crescents that characterize the district, following the design of Thomas Allom. Olsen considers that these schemes were eventually realized. He quotes Hitchcock who finds the development 'the finest Early Victorian layout in London in the semi-urban manner'.

Most of the residents in the further reaches of Holland Park were middle class who could afford the long distance travel to their homes. This may be the reason why we find many mews in this area as well; though not gentry, these middle classes could well afford the horses and carriages needed to get them to and from the City.

Unlike the area around Holland Park, the neighbourhoods near Westbourne and Ladbroke Groves struggled continuously against descending into slum conditions. In *Notting Hill in Bygone Days*, Florence Gladstone discusses a group of streets around Lonsdale Road (near Westbourne Grove) in the 1860s and '70s. 'This group of streets included several cab and omnibus Mews, and the inhabitants were chiefly labourers, horse-keepers and horse-feeders, with a shifting mass of those sorry folk who have come down and down in the world till their home is a loft in some mews patronized by cabmen.' She goes on to note that 'all the elements were present for the development of the degraded conditions of today'. (The book was published in 1924.)

In 1862 there was a 'Ragged School' (the Victorians did not mince words—the poor were not 'disadvantaged' for them!) in Lonsdale Mews, now Colville Mews. Although Colville Mews is not in our Notting Hill Walk, it is interesting to visit this mews today, to compare it with both the 'Ragged School' days of the 1860s, and the 'degraded conditions' of 1924. The mews illustrates the amount of time needed to recover from slum conditions. Even today we do not find the polished look of the Kensington and Belgravia mews; some houses are still nearly derelict, others are in the process of being renovated, and still others are already spruced up, complete with burglar alarms. We find in one mews the sort of interesting mixture we will encounter from mews to mews in this area—a neighbourhood of real interest and vitality, with a cosmopolitan flavour and a variety of architectural styles.

The secluded dead-end of Palace Gardens Mews.

NOTTING HILL WALK

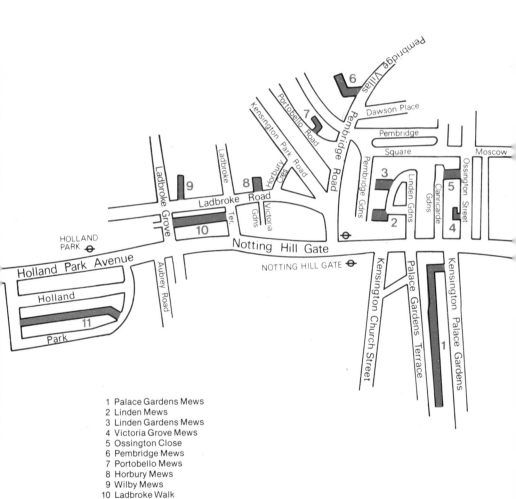

1 Palace Gardens Mews
2 Linden Mews
3 Linden Gardens Mews
4 Victoria Grove Mews
5 Ossington Close
6 Pembridge Mews
7 Portobello Mews
8 Horbury Mews
9 Wilby Mews
10 Ladbroke Walk
11 Holland Park Mews

We start this walk with one of the most splendid examples of an original mews left in London. **Palace Gardens Mews** is so well hidden and little known that the police constable guarding Kensington Palace Gardens, through which it is reached, did not know of its existence. Palace Gardens Mews used to start at Notting Hill Gate, and most modern maps of London still show this; but since the construction of the Czechoslovak embassy in 1968–9 (a grim, monolithic building totally out of place here), the entrance to the mews is at No 25, Kensington Palace Gardens. The embassy, which arrogantly blocks the former entrance to the mews, was designed by three Czech architects in association with Sir Robert Matthew.

This mews, situated on the Kensington Crown Estate, was designed in 1844 by John Marriott Blashfield on a site which had been part of the 'wilderness' first laid out by Queen Anne in about 1705; curiously, some of the feeling of a wilderness exists in this mews even today. Blashfield, who is described in the Post Office Directory as an artist, but was really a manufacturer of tessellated pavements, erected twelve stables in the mews and removed them as far as possible from the grand front houses. The annual ground rents for the stables ranged from £4 to £7 10s per annum, and they were leased to him for a term expiring in 1942. He had little time to benefit from these long leases, however, as he went bankrupt three years later.

Enter the gates of Kensington Palace Gardens, a tree-lined avenue of stately mansions mostly built between 1844 and 1860, which used to be popularly known as 'Millionaire's Row', and which leads to Kensington Palace, birthplace of Queen Victoria. Our mews, serving Millionaire's Row, is surprisingly modest, being very much like a country lane; there are many trees above the garden wall on its west side. The long, winding row of unpainted brick cottages looks like many of the early mews photographs, except that this one has a quiet country feeling rather than the overcrowded city-slum feeling suggested by the earlier pictures. There are many original doors and hardware; and wall plaques denoting the limits of parishes bear the dates 1845 and 1855. The mews gets progressively greener and more secluded as you reach its dead-end.

The reason that these exclusively situated cottages, unlike most of the other mews properties we have seen, have not been renovated or turned into little showplaces seems to be that most of the mansions in Millionaire's Row, along with their mews cottages, have been taken over by foreign embassies. They appear to be using them for offices, storage and garaging, uses which do not call for a showy exterior. From that point of view the embassy occupancy is fortuitous for the mews explorer, but unfortunately in the present jittery climate the occupants are extremely suspicious of passers-by in this quiet street and may challenge your right to walk there. No one, including Kensington Borough Council in whose borough the mews lies, seems to be quite sure what legal rights a walker there has; however, the Royal Borough of Kensington and Chelsea themselves produce a walk booklet which includes Kensington Palace Gardens,

The little known Palace Gardens Mews, built on the site of Queen Anne's 'wilderness'.

and there are no gates between this and the mews. It is a private road on which you are permitted to walk, but if challenged, you should probably leave.

Now cross Notting Hill Gate and proceed to Linden Gardens, following it around to the left where you will find the grand arch to **Linden Mews**. The arch was built in about 1875 and spans one corner of the square court around which the unrestored cottages are grouped. This mews, like the earlier one we saw, gives us a chance to see what mews buildings looked like before renovation, extension or elaborate repair. During our visit we even encountered the obligatory washing fluttering in the breeze, which seems so often to be present in slum photographs. The ownership of the arch is not known.

Continue along Linden Gardens, which once formed the smallest parcel of the Ladbroke Estate, until you reach **Linden Gardens Mews**, also

Linden Garden Mews.

built in about 1875, and known as Chater Mews until 1911. Here too we have buildings grouped around a yard, but these have been thoroughly restored and whitewashed. The yard has an attractive brick paving, and No 3 has a boot-scraper and one of the rare stable doors with top and bottom divisions. The rural peace of the interior courtyard is jarred every few minutes by the sound of underground trains which surface close by, but fortunately not within sight of the mews.

Turning left into Notting Hill Gate and left again into Ossington Street, we reach **Victoria Grove Mews,** an L-shaped street with freshly painted houses, and overhanging trees at its dead-end. The mews is shown but not named in the 1847 map of Paddington. Continuing along Ossington Street and glancing into mews—like **Ossington Close** (before 1925 called Leinster Mews and Palace Court Livery Stables)—we turn left into Moscow Road and Pembridge Square, and right into Pembridge Villas.

59

Pembridge Mews.

Horbury Mews.

The cluttered foreign look of Holland Park Mews (1980).

Across the road is the long lane which holds you in suspense until the corner is turned to reveal **Pembridge Mews**, two rows of cottages and a cobbled road surface with two curving runnels converging into one in the centre. This mews was built in 1849–51 by William Cullingford. The name Pembridge was given to these streets by William Kinnaird Jenkins, whose father leased this site from the Ladbroke family; Jenkins named them after towns and villages in his native Herefordshire.

Now we walk back on Pembridge Villas to Portobello Road and **Portobello Mews**, another group of mostly unrestored cottages situated around a central yard. Evidence of the nearby antique market appears in some of the ornaments and bric-a-brac displayed here. Portobello got its name from the Porto Bello farmhouse on this site, whose owner named it following the British capture of Porto Bello from the Spaniards in 1739.

Continue south on Pembridge Road, turning into Ladbroke Road until you reach **Horbury Mews** on your right. This unusual mews was built on the site of a former nurseryman's ground in 1877, many years after houses in Ladbroke Road were built by William Chadwick, one of the principal architects of the Ladbroke Estate. This grouping of late Victorian structures is ranged along three sides of a large, cobbled yard, and the wide interior space, coupled with the size of the buildings, gives this mews unusual grandeur. For once the life of the researcher is made easy by the clear dating of the main structure as 1878. Note the keystone brick detail above all the arched windows, and the contrast between the less altered west side and the modernized east side, where dormers have been added. No 8 is especially favoured in its secluded position.

Now continue along Ladbroke Road to **Wilby Mews** with the Ladbroke Arms, established in 1843, at its entrance. There, on fine days, lunch-time drinkers can watch the comings and goings in the mews from the pub's flower-lined outdoor terrace. No 17 at the mews' entrance is appropriately named 'The Little House'. The mews is a mixture of restored brick façades and original cottages, and No 13 is an example of the clever use of space with its interior courtyard created by a brick wall entered through an arched iron gate. A plaque on the side of No 12 gives the date of 1845. Wilby Mews appears on the first Ordnance Survey map of 1865 but is not mentioned in the Post Office Directory until much later. The name is probably connected with Benjamin Wilby of Soho Square, who was involved in several development schemes in this area in the early nineteenth century.

Now retrace your steps to Ladbroke Terrace, walking south a short distance to **Ladbroke Walk**, until 1939 known as Ladbroke Terrace Mews, which contains a number of interesting mews houses. Emerging from Ladbroke Walk proceed south and cross Holland Park Avenue, turning left into Holland Park and right into **Holland Park Mews**. This very unusual mews appears unnamed on the Ordnance Survey map of 1865, and was probably completed by that year. It was built by the brothers William and Francis Radford and is remarkable for the careful attention given to the design of its coach-houses and stables. The *Survey* points out that details such as the stucco mouldings on the chimneys and the balusters are similar to the villas themselves. The widely proportioned windows (five horizontal by four vertical panes), the external stairs leading to the living accommodation on the first floor, and the crowning cornices topped by elegant balustrades are details not usually found in mews cottages. The clutter of the innumerable outside stairways gives the mews an interesting, somewhat foreign look.

The freeholds of the first mews houses here were sold in 1860 for prices ranging from £87 to £147; thirty years later, No 54 was sold for £1,050 showing how quickly these houses appreciated in value. At the time of our visit, a similar three-bedroomed cottage was fetching exactly a hundred times the 1891 price.

Continue to the end of the mews to inspect the splendid arch, one of the three-arched variety based on the design of a triumphal arch, having side entrances for pedestrians. A report by the Town Planning Committee of April 1978 warns of a crack in this arch, but at the time of our visit, two years later, nothing much had been done about this crack. Passing through the arch cautiously and looking for signs of falling plaster, those wishing to continue with our next walk can now amble through Holland Park, inspecting what is left of the old Holland House (now a youth hostel) and proceed to Kensington High Street.

Holland Park Mews (1974). Note the external stairs, roof balustrades and widely proportioned windows.

The South Transept, Great Exhibition (1851). (H. Bibby after Mayall)

Kensington

Below : A procession of visitors to the Great Exhibition of 1851 (Richard Doyle).
An omnibus to the Great Exhibition, 1851 (Cruikshank).

THE rural hamlet of Kensington, one hour from London on horse-back, was far enough away to serve as a refuge for those fleeing from the Great Plague of 1665. In the late seventeenth century King William III, who disliked London because of its dampness and its custom of dining in public, decided to buy the Earl of Nottingham's house in Kensington, which came to be known as Kensington Palace. The royal presence attracted notables as well as shop-keepers and artisans and transformed the country village into a significant suburb of London.

Leigh Hunt, the celebrated nineteenth-century chronicler of the *Old Court Suburb* writes glowingly of Kensington's past:

> There is not a step of the way, from . . . Kensington Gore to . . . Holland House, in which you are not greeted with the face of some pleasant memory. Here, to 'mind's eyes' . . . stands a beauty, looking out of a window; there, a wit, talking with other wits at a garden gate; there, a poet on the green sward, glad to get out of the London smoke and find himself among trees. Here comes De Veres of the time of old; Hollands and Davenants, of the Stuart and Cromwell times; Evelyn peering about him soberly, and Samuel Pepys in a bustle . . . Here, in his carriage, is King William the Third, going from the Palace to open Parliament . . . and there, from out of Kensington Gardens, comes bursting, as if the whole recorded polite world were in flower at one and the same period, all the fashion of the gayest times of those sovereigns, blooming with chintzes, full-blown with hoop-petticoats, towering top-knots and toupees . . . Who is to know of all this company, and not be willing to meet it?

At the beginning of the nineteenth century, Kensington was still rural enough to allow Mr Wilberforce, a resident at Gore House from 1808 to 1821, the observation that he could admire 'the beauties of nature as if I were two hundred miles from the great city'. Between 1841 and 1871, however, Kensington Town (excluding Brompton) experienced a five-fold population increase to over 91,000. Some of this influx may have been due to the Great Exhibition of 1851 on a site in Hyde Park, the purpose of which was to present a living picture of the point of development at which mankind had arrived. The Commissioners for the Exhibition of 1851, a group of illustrious persons having Prince Albert himself as their president, were organized to administer the exhibition and the land south of the site, upon which institutions furthering the aims of the exhibition were to be built.

Notwithstanding the royal sponsorship of the exhibition, the residents of the new houses facing the park strenuously opposed it, foreseeing a 'constant stream of hooligans'. And indeed this disruption of their quiet life is aptly described by Leigh Hunt in his *Old Court Suburb*: 'There certainly has been a dust and kick about the once quiet approach to Kensington, a turmoil of crowds, and omnibuses, and cabs, of hot faces and loud voices, of stalls, dogs, penny trumpets, policemen, and extempore public houses, which . . . one could hardly have wished to see continued.'

What the exclusive residents did not perhaps foresee, was the extent of the estate belonging to the Commissioners, who used the proceeds of the exhibition and parliamentary funds to acquire it. They, in turn, began selling it to builders and speculators, whose activity is described by the *Building News* of 1859: '. . . amongst the great speculative builders who are now expending almost fabulous amounts of capital, none were more important than [Charles James] Freake, [William] Jackson, and [Charles] Aldin, who, within the last two or three years, have erected buildings of a most princely character. In fact, these gentlemen with a fearless speculative energy may be said conjointly to have created a new town composed of dwelling houses of a highly superior class, that for splendour of detail and internal conveniences more than rival the palazzi of the nobles of Venice . . .'

It goes without saying that all this building could not be accomplished without some destruction of Kensington's rural character. Miss Thackeray, another Kensington chronicler, saw 'the hawthorn bleed as it is laid low and is transformed year after year into iron railings and areas, for particulars of which you are requested to apply to the railway company, and to Mr Taylor, the house agent'.

As we have seen previously, a generous number of mews were built to attract a good class of buyers. The *Survey of London* examines an area from Prince's Gate Mews to the top of Queen's Gate which fell mostly on the estates of the Earls of Harrington, the Alexander family, the Commissioners of 1851, and the Trustees of Mills' Charity. Here some 670 houses were built, and additionally some 480 coach-houses and stables. The *Survey* continues with its description: 'At the rear of the houses were the ranges of two-storeyed mews providing coach-houses and stables below and coachmen's accommodation above, these simple brick structures being screened from the street behind imposing arches which continued the character of the flanking terraces. The cobbled courts were sometimes at a lower level than the street (that is, two or three feet above the basement floors of the houses). In many cases, especially in Aldin's developments, the flues from each mews building are gathered into a large arched structure, taking the form of a flying buttress, and carried up to the top of the rear wall of the main house, presumably in order to prevent smoke from the mews entering the upper windows of the house.' Not many examples of this interesting architectural feature remain.

But the speculators in Kensington, just as elsewhere, may have been too optimistic about the demand for their houses. Olsen considers that Kensington had never seriously threatened the pre-eminence of Belgravia, much less of Mayfair; and by the late Victorian period was being deserted by the large, prosperous and respectable families for whom it was intended. He quotes the *Estates Gazette* of 1878 which reports that builders were forced to subdivide the big houses for multiple occupation. The *Survey*, in describing one of Freake's developments, comments that 'enough, or more than enough, stables were provided for everyone of the thirty-one houses Freake actually built'. In another place, the *Survey* points out that in 1888 'a layout was changed by agreed omission of an intended mews'.

Olsen cites as indirect evidence of the deterioration of this area the fact that some 'drivers of shop-carts or cabwashers' now appeared in the mews which had originally been intended for private servants. As we know now, Kensington did not slide very far, and the comment in Booth's *Life and Labour of the People of London* in 1899 perhaps still stands today: '. . . the dominant population of Kensington and Brompton was a middle class verging on fashion and wealth.'

With this kind of population, Kensington becomes one of the most fruitful areas in London for mews exploration. Not quite central enough to have fallen prey to commercial pressures, and not quite fashionable enough to command Belgravia and Mayfair prices, many of the Kensington mews have retained the social mix which makes for a stimulating city environment. Here we find mews ranging from the most quaint to the downright shabby; elaborate, touching or laughable attempts to dress up mews façades in Walk One give way to simple, unadorned brick cottages, in some cases only a step away from slum conditions, in Walk Two.

Flue-arches, Queen's Gate Gardens.

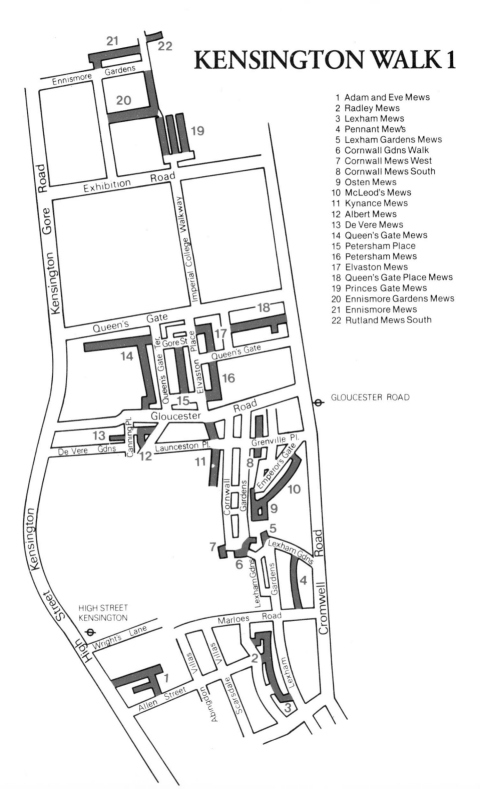

KENSINGTON WALK 1

1 Adam and Eve Mews
2 Radley Mews
3 Lexham Mews
4 Pennant Mews
5 Lexham Gardens Mews
6 Cornwall Gdns Walk
7 Cornwall Mews West
8 Cornwall Mews South
9 Osten Mews
10 McLeod's Mews
11 Kynance Mews
12 Albert Mews
13 De Vere Mews
14 Queen's Gate Mews
15 Petersham Place
16 Petersham Mews
17 Elvaston Mews
18 Queen's Gate Place Mews
19 Princes Gate Mews
20 Ennismore Gardens Mews
21 Ennismore Mews
22 Rutland Mews South

We start our walking tour on Kensington High Street, from which we enter the gateway to **Adam and Eve Mews**, situated between two shoe shops. On this site stood the Adam and Eve pub which gave its name to the mews. Here, according to Moore's Diary, Sheridan used to stop regularly for a dram on his way to Holland House, running up a long bill which Lord Holland had to pay. (Leigh Hunt tells us that 'a servant was regularly in attendance—at Holland House—all night; partly to furnish, we believe, a bottle of champagne to the thirsty Sheridan in case he should happen to call for one betwixt his slumbers'; but also, adds Leigh Hunt slyly, to 'secure the bed curtains from being set on fire by his candle'.)

Once we enter this extensive and interesting mews, we leave city traffic and shoppers far behind. We are at once confronted by a great variety of styles and façades, and observe the cross-brick patterns running along the roof-lines, and the small square cobbling of the paving. The sprinkling of commercial establishments in the first arm of the mews could be responsible for the modern undistinguished street lamps we find here; perhaps it was felt that this stretch of the mews did not deserve the attractive lanterns we find later on. Some of the standpipes here bear the name of Thomas Crapper, popularizer of the water closet.

We pass No 27 with its nicely pointed gable and arched window, before this part of the mews ends in the Royal Navy Provost building. The Post Office Directory of 1889 locates the headquarters of the West London Rifles (4th Middlesex) here, but the mews was in existence before then, appearing as Adam and Eve Cottages on the first Ordnance Survey map of 1865. Turning right from this lane, the decorative iron hinges and ornamental trees of No 36 come into view. The house opposite has another of the pointed gables, unusual in a mews building, and No 60, tucked away near the end, has a plaque showing Adam and Eve under the apple tree. Apple Tree Cottage, as it is called, was sold in 1950 for a mere £7500, being described by the agents as a 'small, detached house, containing 5/6 bedrooms, 2 reception rooms and 2 baths'.

Leaving the mews by way of Allen Street and walking south to Stratford Road, turn left and glance into mews-like Stratford Studios. Cross over into **Radley Mews**, observing the balconied first storey and following its zig-zag course into **Lexham Mews**. The long run and adjoining gardens make these two mews an especially quiet street.

Exit through the well-worn red brick arch, built in about 1870, turning left into Lexham Gardens and right into Marloes Road, which leads you to **Pennant Mews**. Walk through this mews, noting the pattern above the window arches, and proceed north along Lexham Gardens to **Lexham Gardens Mews**, whose name was approved in 1884. Continue through Lexham Walk into **Cornwall Gardens Walk**, until 1948 called Cornwall Gardens Stables. The village-style intersection of lanes converging at odd angles enhances the rural aspect of this mews. Continuing to the left, one may observe the amusing combination of prominent drainpipes and leaded lights. This block has been altered and extended upwards, but the

The Adam and Eve public house, which gave the mews its name, photographed in the 1890s. *Right :* Adam and Eve Mews.

The village-style intersection of Cornwall Gardens Walk.

Cornwall Mews South, showing a combination of drainpipes and leaded lights.

identifying characteristics of a mews are still visible: cobbles, upper-floor external doors, the former low roof-line, coach-house and stable hardware, and of course the arch at its end. According to the 1847 tithe map for Kensington this mews, as well as Cornwall Mews West and South, and Kynance Mews which follow, were on the estate of Thomas Broadwood who, however, may not have been responsible for its development.

Emerging from this arch, we immediately see another one with a small pedestrian arch to its west. The arch, built in about 1870, forms the entrance to the short cul-de-sac of **Cornwall Mews West**, where, at the time of our visit, a grand cocktail party was in progress on the roofs of the little houses. Proceeding along Cornwall Gardens and turning south on Grenville Place, we pass the arches dividing the two sections of **Cornwall Mews South**. Bebbington traces this area's Cornwall names (including

Right: Osten Mews.

Kynance, which is a place in Cornwall) to the Reverend Samuel Walker of Cornwall; he is the same ill-fated clergyman whose ruinous speculations we have already encountered in Notting Hill. It is, however, more likely that these mews were named after the Duke of Cornwall and Prince of Wales (later Edward VII), who came of age in 1862.

The western part of this mews was formerly called Cornwall Mews West, and both sections appear on the Ordnance Survey map of 1865, which is also the date Anne Riches gives for the construction of the arches. We continue south to Emperor's Gate, leading to **Osten Mews**. This and McLeod's Mews which follows it were part of the eastern limb of Lord Kensington's estate which, according to Anne Riches, was isolated from the main body of the estate by the construction of the Circle Line. The area was not developed until the 1870s, when the handsome red brick arch was also built.

Osten Mews is a round complex of lanes, with the unusual circular staircase of No 9 (demolished since our photograph was taken) in one curve, and the elaborately restored, purple-trimmed No 15 in another. Some of these mews dwellers are condemned to look out at the West London Air Terminal. More high-rises confront the eye on emerging from this mews into **McLeod's Mews**, now only a fragment. A notice on the fence shielding the large building plot on the site of the former Nos 1–7 called the attention of residents to a local inquiry which was to decide the appeal by the developers against the Borough of Kensington's decision to refuse them planning permission. Since this is not in a conservation area, the demolition of these houses evidently did not require any permission, but the construction of two tower blocks apparently does.

Now backtrack to Grenville Place until you come to the arches marking the entrance to the two sections of **Kynance Mews**. This was known as Cornwall Mews until 1924, when the Council decided to make life a little easier for the postmen. The arches were built in about 1860, and we enter the western one first to inspect this section; here one can easily forget London and imagine oneself in a quiet village deep in the English countryside. Most of one side is taken up by a churchyard wall, against which the mews dwellers have placed statues, flowers, and potted plants, some of them hung from hooks taken from the former stables on the site. Bell Cottage is notable for its chimney and leaded lights, and the vicarage cottage at the end is suitably quaint. A Kynance Mews resident in her nineties clearly remembers an ageing groom called Smithers, who related what happened here in the early part of the century. A runaway horse and carriage, driven by Smithers at high speed down Victoria Road plunged into the mews over the churchyard wall. The place of impact on the wall is still evident, marked by slightly newer bricks near the steps to Victoria Road. The same resident also recalls communicating doors between the front houses in Cornwall Gardens and the Kynance cottages. Because of the narrow space between Cornwall Gardens and Kynance Mews, the mews cottages extend to a depth of merely one small room.

Telephone 3859, Western.

CARR & CO

- Cars for Hire. • Engineering & Coach Repairs.
- All Motor Accessories. • Painting, Upholstering, Cape Hoods, Wings, Bonnets, Radiators, Windscreens, Plating. • All Orders receive prompt attention. • Agents for the Car and General Corporation, Ltd.

Emperor's Gate Garage & Motor Works

4 and 5, McLEOD'S MEWS,

EMPEROR'S GATE,

CROMWELL ROAD, S.W.

An advertisement in the official Kensington Guide for 1914.

Left : Kynance Mews, western section. *Above :* Ennismore Mews.

Now enter the eastern arm of Kynance Mews, dominated by the tower of Imperial College in the background. It was the arch to this section which had attached to it, at the time of our visit, the plea to find its owner which we reproduce on page 135. Walk through this mews and north along Gloucester Road to Victoria Grove and **Albert Mews**. This is interesting for its row of balconied cottages, with the living accommodation above the former coach-houses reached from the outside stairs to the balconies. The mews appears in Wheeler & Davis's Survey of 1846. Now backtrack to Gloucester Road and continue to Canning Place and **De Vere Mews**, named for Aubrey de Vere, a Norman nobleman who possessed vast estates including the manor of Kensington.

De Vere Mews is listed as being of architectural and historical interest, as it is one of the very few mews of its type left in London. It has a similar layout to John Nash's Carlton Mews, where carriaging was on the ground floor and stabling was reached by a ramp leading to the first floor. In De Vere Mews the accommodation was above the stabling, and the mews was used until very recently for its original purpose, as shown in the photograph opposite. Writing about Carlton Mews in *Country Life* Mark Girouard describes the Duke of Leinster's former stable there being converted into an enormous sitting room, with cars in the relative dark down below, and wonders why this successful conversion could not be allowed to stand. In the event, Carlton Mews did not survive the architecturally destructive climate of the 1950s. Being forced to retain the basic layout of De Vere Mews, the present developers decided to use every inch

The balconied cottages of Albert Mews.

De Vere Mews in 1973 (*right*) and in 1980 (*below*).

The interior court of De Vere Cottages.

of space they could find, including the relatively dark ground floor coach-house area. They created a warren of office and residential spaces, a kind of ghetto for the rich, in which elegant Kensingtonians are to live and work together in a space as confined as that allotted to some of their poorer fellow mews dwellers in the nineteenth century. However, mews explorers may be thankful for having such a fine example available for inspection.

Almost next door (on the other side of De Vere Gardens) is a similar galleried mews grouped around an interior courtyard, but lighter and more airy, which is now known as **De Vere Cottages**, but formerly went under the name of Laconia Mews (and perhaps also Canning Place Mews). There is some nice paving and statuary in the courtyard, and an assortment of leaded lights and fake door hinges is scattered throughout the mews. It was built in 1875 and converted to residential use in 1921.

Leaving De Vere Cottages, we cross Gloucester Road to **Queen's Gate Mews**, roughly L-shaped, which contains well over a quarter of a mile of former stabling and shows how extensive the Kensington mews could be.

Petersham Place (1972).

The north–south arm is worth exploring as it leads past the site of Jacob Epstein's former studio, and there are examples of unchanged houses in Nos 5 and 7. A look in the vintage car showroom at the exit of the mews may alleviate the fatigue induced by its length. The *Survey* dates the origin of this mews as about 1858.

Continue via Gore Street to **Petersham Place** on the former Harrington Estate, known until 1939 as Queen's Gate Terrace Mews. It gets its name from the earls of Harrington, whose subsidiary title was Viscount Petersham. The arch, built in the late 1850s, is held by Anne Riches to be without the architectural panache of the other arches in the vicinity. Though many of the houses here have had dormer additions, some of them still retain the original first-floor external doors.

Continue via Petersham Lane to **Petersham Mews**, where at the time of our visit No 3, a two-bedroomed house, was being offered for £89,500. Continue into **Elvaston Mews**, noting the sign above No 11 announcing stables for Rothmans of Pall Mall. Its arch, built in about 1865, is similar to the splendid arch of **Queen's Gate Place Mews**, which is a little out of our way. It is strongly classical, with Ionic fluted columns supporting a broken pediment. Both of these arches may have been constructed by the same speculative builder, working on the estate of the 1851 Commissioners. The name Elvaston probably comes from Elvaston Castle in Derbyshire, the seat of the Earl of Harrington, another of the Kensington property owners.

Now cross Queen's Gate for the long trek down the Imperial College Walkway, stopping to glance at the tower which we have already encountered in background views. This tower, although now at the centre of Imperial College, is historically the tower of the old Imperial Institute, the rest of the building having been demolished. Cross Exhibition Road to enter the unpromising gateway to **Princes Gate Mews**, a three-pronged mews of great interest. First turn right and into its southern arm, lined by elegant town houses on both sides. During our visit, a large scaffold on one of the houses indicated the upward extension by its owners. Walk back to the centre arm, with more substantial houses, and traverse the passage next to cranberry-coloured No 53 to reach the northern arm, where the unity of the mews is broken by the modern addition to the Imperial College. One may wonder whether Princess Margaret, who opened this sterile building on 8 October 1963 gave a thought to the contrast between this bleak symbol of technology and the frail beauty of the mews houses which stood here until the technologically perfected

Princes Gate Mews.

The classical arch that marks the entrance to Queen's Gate Place Mews.

A side arm of Princes Gate Mews with the Victoria and Albert Museum in the background.

Ennismore Gardens Mews.

wrecker's ball easily reduced them to rubble. One may also be permitted to wonder whether the aim stated in the College's annual report for 1955–6 that the new buildings 'would not be modern in the vulgar sense that they will astonish our neighbours and clash with pleasant legacies of the past' has been realized.

This legacy can be traced to Charles James Freake, a builder who allowed an unusual amount of space in the layout of this mews complex in 1859. He could perhaps not have foreseen that the conservation area line was going to run through the centre of the mews' northern arm, thus dooming the northernmost row. Follow this arm now, leading to **Ennismore Gardens Mews**, roughly L-shaped, which in April 1980 gained some unaccustomed notoriety when a Libyan was shot down at the door to his office in what the newspapers described as 'the secluded, cobbled mews'. Inspect the north-leading arm, noting the keystone detail above the windows and former arched doorways which we have seen in Horbury Mews of later vintage. The east-leading arm is across from a small park, and all the buildings in its single south-facing row are handsome. The arch to the eastern entrance of the mews is considered by Anne Riches to be one of the finest examples of mews façades in London. This splendid arch is another waif, looking for its owner.

Emerging through the Corinthian columns, one soon reaches **Ennismore Mews** with the Ennismore Arms at its corner, and the view dominated by the steeple of the Russian Orthodox Cathedral. The ground occupied by Ennismore Gardens, Place and Street belonged to the 'bigamous duchess of Kingston', whose Kingston House, built in 1770, stood in Kensington Road. This duchess, according to Leigh Hunt, was an adventuress, who married one husband (the Earl of Bristol) when he was just out of his teens, and another one (the Duke, nephew of Lady Mary Wortley Montagu) who appears 'never to have outgrown the teens of his understanding'. Her ladyship's maxim was to be 'short, clear, and surprising; she concentrated her rhetoric into swearing and dressed in a style next to nakedness'. Be that as it may—Leigh Hunt always delighted in spreading a bit of scandalous gossip—Kingston House later became the home of the earls of Listowel, also known as the viscounts Ennismore, who remained there until 1937. The mews first appears in Westminster rate books in 1849.

Continuing now along Ennismore Street, **Rutland Mews South** appears on the right. Here, on the fine spring day of our visit, children were paddling in inflatable pools, set up in the short T-shaped branches of the mews, and a small dog was snapping at intruders. **Rutland Mews West** which faces this block, consists of only one rather grand house with a prominent clock. Both mews are named after Rutland House, the former Knightsbridge mansion which became the town house of the Dukes of Rutland and on whose grounds Rutland Street, Mews, and Gardens were built. Here we end our walk in one of the most elegant sections of central London.

KENSINGTON WALK 2

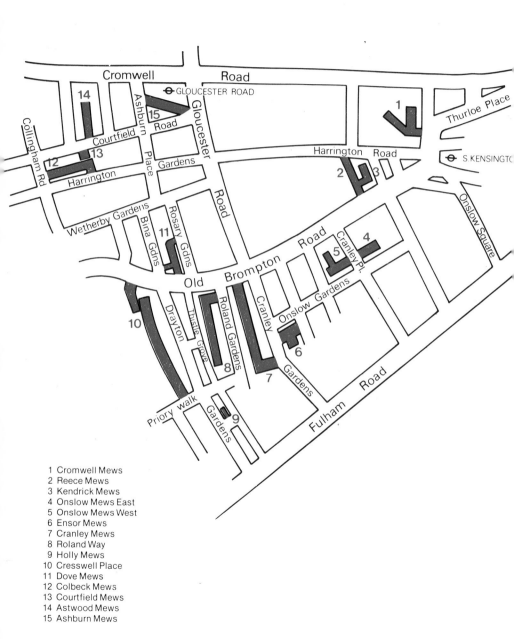

1 Cromwell Mews
2 Reece Mews
3 Kendrick Mews
4 Onslow Mews East
5 Onslow Mews West
6 Ensor Mews
7 Cranley Mews
8 Roland Way
9 Holly Mews
10 Cresswell Place
11 Dove Mews
12 Colbeck Mews
13 Courtfield Mews
14 Astwood Mews
15 Ashburn Mews

Starting at South Kensington Tube station, we immediately plunge into the two-pronged **Cromwell Mews**, which is reasonably well preserved, considering its proximity to Cromwell Road and the heart of South Kensington. As always with a mews, we must marvel how quickly we can feel remote from the big city, literally only a few steps from the busiest roads. The mews was built by Charles James Freake, whom we encountered in the previous walk, although this mews is much more modest than Princes Gate Mews. In 1866–7, the years when Cromwell Mews was built, Freake employed nearly 400 men in his building operations, making him one of the largest builders in London. Henry Browne Alexander, to whose estate Cromwell Mews belonged, was a distant descendant by marriage of John Thurloe, secretary and intimate friend of Oliver Cromwell.

We continue along Harrington Road, where we soon enter **Reece Mews** on our left. This, and the adjoining **Kendrick Mews**, are busy little lanes with working garages and small businesses, perhaps giving us more of the flavour of the working nineteenth-century mews than many of the fancy residential mews in our previous walk. The mews was named for Robert Reece of Barbados, whose wife Louisa inherited some gardens and cottages on this site. Robert Reece arranged to develop the land in 1869, and in a complex transaction, involving the neighbouring Alexander and Mills' Charity estates, our old friend Charles Freake undertook the construction. To make the transaction even more complicated, Freake exchanged some land with another builder, Matthew Scott, who allowed Freake to build both sides of Reece Mews in exchange for building Kendrick Mews.

After proceeding along Old Brompton Road and Cranley Place, we come upon the two sections of Onslow Mews. Glancing first into **Onslow Mews East** as a means of comparison, we turn our attention to **Onslow Mews West**, a genuinely unrestored mews, even boasting laundry strung across its width during all our visits. Interesting features here are the upper-storey external doors with safety gates, the unadorned brick-facings relieved by flower boxes on almost every window sill, and more standpipes by Thomas Crapper. The mews was part of an 84-acre estate which Alderman Henry Smith left in trust in 1627 to pay pensions to his poorest relations and for the 'relief and ransom of poor captives being slaves under Turkish pirates'. One of the trustees of Smith's Charity was Viscount Cranley, eldest son of the Earl of Onslow. Onslow Mews West was built in the 1860s, but the eastern part preceded it by about ten years. The plain arch through which we now exit is one of the rare mews arches of unknown ownership which has recently been restored.

Returning along Cranley Place we turn right into Onslow Gardens, and follow this many-pronged street to its second arm, where we turn south for the interesting arch and façade to **Ensor Mews**, a façade which is unusual in providing rear windows for some of these mews houses. This F-shaped mews, with arches on each end, has a quiet south-leading arm

89

Cromwell Mews.

enhanced by St Peter's Church in the background. The first and shorter arm ends in a wall with overhanging trees. There are perfect cobbles and several unspoiled brick-faced houses. The origin of its unusual name, which was officially approved in 1874, is unknown.

Emerging from the eastern arch, we turn left into Cranley Gardens to find the unpromising back entrance to **Cranley Mews**. As soon as we have turned the corner, however, we behold a long, curving, cobbled lane with low cottages on both sides. Our attention is held immediately by No 26, with its flamboyant posters advertising its private war with Smith's

Cranley Mews.

Laundry fluttering in Onslow Mews West reveals its unchanged character.

Charity estate, which is being accused of corruption in forcing out one of its tenants. One may wonder how either Alderman Smith, with his concern for 'the poorest of my kindred', or Viscount Cranley would have dealt with this affair.

We amble down the length of the mews and leisurely inspect these typical mews cottages, one with a probably original iron circular staircase in its front room. Its name was officially approved in 1878, although building was not completed at that time.

A few steps away we turn into **Roland Way**, whose entrance, dominated

Semi-circular doors are an unusual feature in Roland Way.

Balconied cottages in Dove Mews.

by a petrol station and garage, does not prepare the visitor for the peaceful and unspoiled character of the mews. Especially notable are the rarely seen semi-circular arched stable doors, of which we find many examples here. The mews was called Alveston Mews until 1921, and Roland Mews until 1936. The present name may be connected with Anne Elizabeth Rolland from Paris, who was involved in a number of Kensington building ventures in the 1860s. We walk the length of the mews and can barely notice that half of its western row consists of a motor parts shop, because the building is almost totally hidden by a thick covering of ivy. Turning right into the hidden exit of the mews (no public right of way, but usually open), we cross over to Thistle Grove, a pleasant, garden-lined walkway, which we pursue to **Holly Mews**. This short, bright cul-de-sac has such small cottages that their external stairs and balconies may well have been originally built as a space saving device.

Turning north along Drayton Gardens and left into Priory Walk, we come upon **Creswell Place**, a long, open and wide mews with some outstanding cottages. One of these, No 22, half-tiled and gabled, was being offered for £110,000 during our visit. No 17–16, with the 1894 date inscribed in its pediment, has unfortunately been spoiled by an enormous modern glass front. This mews was called Bolton Mews until 1908, when it got its present designation, presumably after the oddly named judge Sir Cresswell Cresswell, a Kensington resident in the mid-nineteenth century. We continue along Cresswell Place which gradually loses its mews character, and cross Brompton Road into Bina Gardens and the entrance to **Dove Mews**.

This most unusual mews, built on the site of Dove Lane by John Spicer, a builder of Pimlico, has one entire balconied row. There are stairs only at either end of the long-running balcony, so that the balcony is (or rather was, as some of the present cottages have entrances at ground floor level) shared by all the mews dwellers. No 10 has been turned into a 'quaint' little country cottage.

We continue northwards, turning left into Harrington Gardens where we find the entrance to **Colbeck Mews**. Although only the northern row contains mews cottages, the houses here are of a good size and boast five gables, each one a different shape. The mews was possibly named after a Kensington landowner, the Reverend William Colbeck, and this name was officially approved in 1875. We exit through the triumphal arch, a rather more elaborate structure than the usual arch found on this (Gunter) estate. The arch was in the process of being restored on the day of our visit.

Turning right twice we reach the entrances to two mews, **Courtfield Mews** to the south, and **Astwood Mews** to the north. Courtfield Mews, a pleasant courtyard of whitewashed, balconied cottages, has only the stump of its arch remaining. Unlike Dove Mews, the balcony here is no longer used for access. This mews was built in about 1870.

Astwood Mews, which also lost its arch, is totally different. It contains highly unusual mews houses, all of them with unadorned, perhaps even grimy façades of typically Victorian brickwork. All of them have peaked roofs and are in pretty original condition. The mews consists almost entirely of working garages, which may not be ideal for its private residents, but provide the bustle of ceaseless mews activity which was so common in former days.

The mews was named for Astwood in Bucks, the residence of John Thurloe Brace (step-grandson of Cromwell's secretary John Thurloe), who owned the Kensington estates which were developed by his own great-grandson, John Alexander.

Walking back to Ashburn Place and turning north, we behold the sad spectacle of the former, and still cobbled **Ashburn Mews**, built in the 1870s, which, along with its Grade II listed arch, was destroyed a hundred years later. As we have seen in McLeod's Mews, the developers are always anxious to send in the bulldozers before anyone can stop them. Once they have demolished all the houses on a site, they can rest easy, and years often elapse before anything else rises on the site. With Ashburn Mews we reach the Gloucester Road Tube station and the end of this walk.

NORTH EAST SIDE OF BELGRAVE SQUARE, PIMLICO.
TO LORD BELGRAVE, THIS PLATE IS MOST RESPECTFULLY INSCRIBED
Published Nov. 15, 1828, by Jones & Co. Temple of the Muses, Finsbury Square, London.

Belgravia

BELGRAVE CHAPEL, AND WEST SIDE OF BELGRAVE SQUARE.

THIS 'most aristocratic' area, as many writers about London refer to Belgravia, gets its name from Belgrave in Cheshire, where the Grosvenors hold an estate. The Belgravia lands came into the Grosvenors' hands through the 1677 marriage with heiress Mary Davies, which we discussed earlier. Unlike Mayfair, however, the Grosvenors waited to develop this area until George IV chose nearby Buckingham House as his palace in the 1820s. With their usual luck, the Grosvenors thus possessed another fashionable and lucrative site, leading the author of *The Great Landlords of London* in 1888 to exclaim with heavy sarcasm: 'In the ranks of English dukes there is one whose name stands prominently and pre-eminently associated in the English mind with wealth in London land. What Michelangelo is among artists, Napoleon among generals, Nelson among admirals, such is Hugh Lupus Grosvenor, K.G., P.C., Duke of Westminster, among the noble ground landlords of our metropolis.'

Before the early nineteenth century, this area, known as 'The Five Fields', was a desolate place, through which ran the Westbourne Brook, crossed by 'Bloody Bridge', probably known by that name because of the robberies and violence committed there. Mrs Gascoigne's description of the site is quoted in Augustus Hare's *Walks in London* (1901):

A marshy spot, where not one patch of green
no stunted shrub, nor sickly flower is seen.

In 1825 the builder and developer Thomas Cubitt negotiated with the Grosvenors and the Lowndes family for the right to develop their estates. Cubitt was the son of a carpenter, and himself started as a carpenter. He was highly thought of by everyone, from his workers to the estate owners, and an obituary in *The Builder* described him as 'a great builder and a good man'. Queen Victoria noted in her diary that 'a better, kinder-hearted or more simple, unassuming man never breathed', and the above-mentioned Mrs Gascoigne wrote some flowery verse about him. The story is often told how his Pimlico yard caught fire, resulting in £100,000 worth of damage; but instead of being desolate or bankrupt, Cubitt told his men that they would be at work within a week, and personally subscribed £600 toward buying them new tools.

Cubitt started by levelling the ground, digging out the damp clay and burning it into bricks on the site. The job was made more difficult by the low level of this site, of which Timbs reports that 'it has been ascertained that the ground floor of Westbourne Terrace and Hyde Park Gardens is on a level with the attics of Eaton and Belgrave Square'; this low position being responsible for the 'marshy spot' cited in Mrs Gascoigne's poem.

Cubitt shared the financial burden of this great undertaking with three bankers of Swiss extraction, who in turn employed George Bavesi, a brilliant young architect whose life ended prematurely when he fell to his death from a scaffold. Belgrave Square itself was Bavesi's design, and he was proud enough of its south-side to sign his name on the side of the portico above No 37.

Olsen quotes John Britton, who was a great admirer of Belgrave Square,

Two views of Belgrave Square in 1828.

praising the houses as being 'large, lofty, and in every way spacious, with Stuccoed fronts, porches, balustraded balconies, and . . . columns'. But not everyone shared Britton's enthusiasm. The *Building News* in 1857 found Belgravia 'in point of architectural quality . . . only a very few degrees less insipid and uninteresting' than Baker, Harley and Gower Streets. 'There is not much majesty in the modern elevation of Belgravian squares and wide streets', the *Building News* complained the next year. Another critic (W. Weir) would have liked 'less uniformity in the architecture'. He preferred 'individual character in the houses; we do not like to see them merely as parts of an architectural whole, like soldiers who are only parts of a rank.'

The later Victorians were to be even more vehement about the stuccoed fronts, which they considered fraudulent, and hiding the true and individual character of the houses. Still later Augustus Hare called Belgravia (in 1901) 'wholly devoid of interest, and which none would think of visiting unless drawn thither by the claims of society'. We shall have occasion to remember these critics, when we look about Belgravia with open eyes, not blinded by the elegant glitter of its titled inhabitants.

Our walk starts in the Hans Town area of the Cadogan Estate, which was the last of the inner London developments still providing mews to serve the main residential streets. This area, once the site of a large private mansion called The Pavilion, was developed by Henry Holland at the start of the American War of Independence, which was also responsible for impeding the progress of this development. However, leases which started in those early days, seem to have prevented major redevelopment such as the addition of mews, until the 1870s when the leases were falling in. Thus we have the anomaly of mews being built very late in an area developed much earlier than Belgravia. This gave the mews in this area interesting architectural features such as red brick and ornate Victorian decorative details instead of the uniform stucco so despised by the later Victorians.

On the whole (and with the exception of the Hans Town area) the Belgravia mews are perhaps less interesting than those of our other walks. Because of the immensely high prices of the houses here, these mews do not attract (or cannot retain) the diversity which helps to create a socially healthy city environment. Belgravia, elegant and imposing as it may be, suffers from a lack of street life, shops and restaurants: the mews in particular suffer from a great incidence of bad modernizations, in many cases caused by a developer assured of large profits, no matter how he carries out his conversion. Banfield wrote in 1888 that 'speculative builders appear to be preferred on the [Grosvenor] estate before private occupiers', and this may still hold true.

Perhaps both the strength and weakness of Belgravia is summed up in the quotation from Milton, which is inscribed around the walls of St Michael's Church in Belgravia's Chester Square: 'Nothing is here for tears, nothing to wail, nothing but well and fair.'

The Grenadier pub in 1932.

BELGRAVIA WALK

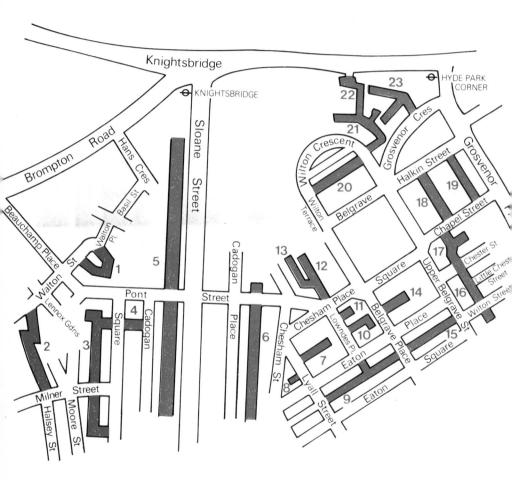

1 Pont Street Mews
2 Lennox Gardens Mews
3 Clabon Mews
4 Shafto Mews
5 Pavilion Road
6 Cadogan Lane
7 Lyall Mews
8 Lyall Mews West

9 Eaton Mews North
10 Lowndes Close
11 Roberts Mews
12 Belgrave Mews West
13 Chesham Mews
14 Belgrave Mews South
15 Eccleston Mews
16 Wilton Mews

17 Groom Place
18 Montrose Place
19 Headfort Place
20 Belgrave Mews North
21 Wilton Row
22 Old Barrack Yard
23 Grosvenor Crescent Mews

Substantial houses in Pont Street Mews.

We start our walk with the unusual **Pont Street Mews**, which can be reached from Knightsbridge Tube station (Hans Crescent exit). Knightsbridge in the early nineteenth century was a shabby, straggling village, famous, however, for its good air. According to ancient legend, two knights travelling from London, quarrelled and fell in mortal combat on the bridge which then gave the whole area its name.

We enter the mews through its only surviving arch, attached to St Saviour's Church, and inscribed with the date 1879. Built of red and brown bricks, its design, according to Anne Riches, is the closest any mews arch comes to a Gothic form. 1879 is one of the latest dates we have for the construction of a mews, and the houses here are truly substantial, with dormer gables, and some hoisting beams protruding. The cobbles and runnels are in fine condition and the houses, with the exception of Nos 12 and 46 with their unnaturally new and false brick-facings and door conversions, are worthy of a closer look. An odd feature of the mews are two

99

chimney stacks with flanking scrolls near the western exit. It is possible that this feature was designed for show, to be seen from Walton Street. The 'Pont' probably comes from the French for bridge, as Pont Street used to bridge the Westbourne Brook.

We leave the mews by its western exit, crossing Pont Street, and reach **Lennox Gardens Mews**, surely one of the most picturesque mews in London. We follow its zigzag course past a French restaurant to find the residential part of the mews, in which the inhabitants have kept parked cars at bay by a liberal display of potted plants along the brick garden wall which forms the west side of the mews. There are many fine examples of not greatly altered and very substantial cottages. The garden wall, so

Lennox Gardens Mews.

reminiscent of Palace Gardens and Kynance Mews, is overhung with trees and variegated ivy, and grass grows between the small square cobbles.

Turning left as we emerge, we come to the wide and cobble-less **Clabon Mews**, at first glance more like an ordinary street than a mews. Nos 13–19 in the southern half are typical mews houses of this area with tall stable doors improved by shiny black paint. Note the arched stable doors of No 18, and the many adjoining cottages showing brick arches in their elevations. The northern half of the mews has many very altered houses, but note the unusual pair at the end, Nos 65 and 67, with four gables echoing the pediment of the Shafto arch opposite. By contrast, the upward extension of No 69 makes nonsense of its peaked roof.

The symmetrical red-brick façade to Shafto Mews.

Moxton Clabon was solicitor to the Cadogan family and was probably involved in building this mews for them in 1875. Perhaps Clabon, like barrister John Eden Shafto, who bestowed his name on the mews opposite, did not realize that his name, given to what was then an insignificant stable yard, would one day grace an important residential street of the metropolis.

Unlike Clabon Mews, which did not occupy a central position on the Cadogan Estate and did not get an arch of its own, **Shafto Mews**, whose arch we now enter, occupied an important position in the heart of the estate. The mews is a short block, ending in a red brick wall with an arch

in relief and a pedestrian gate, through which we shall exit. The arch is part of a symmetrical street façade, containing chimney stacks and flanking scrolls as seen in the odd feature of Pont Street Mews. The two end houses, one of them covered in thick ivy, with their Victorian dormer gables, are worthy of note.

We next proceed along Pont Street, and follow this long and only communicating link between the Cadogan and Grosvenor estates. Bebbington makes the point that the 'pigheadedness' of the early land-owners is strikingly visible on the modern London map. The estate owners

Matching pediments in Eaton Mews North.

were content to develop their own areas, and either neglected, or actively prevented communicating links with other estates. In proceeding to the Grosvenor Estate, we cross two former mews which, though now paved, still contain a number of mews cottages. The first of these is **Pavilion Road**, perhaps in this, its latest name, commemorating Henry Holland's eighteenth-century Pavilion, but formerly called variously New Road, Alfred Place, Chapel Row and Taylor's Cottages. After crossing Sloane Street, we come upon **Cadogan Lane**, formerly Little Cadogan Place, with its odd purple house in the dead-end. We turn into Chesham Place now and follow Lyall Street to **Lyall Mews**.

This two-pronged complex has been less spoiled than some of the other Belgravia mews, being quiet, cobbled and bright, with many of its houses not yet done up to the nines. Charles Lyall and his friend William Lowndes, great-great grandson of the first William Lowndes (a successful financier and politician) built many of the streets in this area. Lyall Mews first appeared in the Westminster rate books in 1843.

We continue now on Lyall Street, glancing into **Lyall Mews West**, whose first few cottages are interesting. Crossing Eaton Place, we encounter the two sections of **Eaton Mews North** with their dissimilar arches. The western section, with its ornate Grosvenor lamp-post, is worth a brief exploration before continuing through the eastern section. No 34 has an unusual pediment echoing the third arch of this mews, through which we now leave, walking north along Lowndes Place.

The two-arched street façade, hiding Roberts Mews and Lowndes Close.

Here we soon note the two pediment-topped arches of **Lowndes Close** and **Roberts Mews**, illustrating nicely the builders' clever way of enhancing the street façades and hiding the mews at the same time. Lowndes Close, called Lowndes Mews until 1938, has some nice cottages, but the overall feeling here is more Belgravia than former stable block. Roberts Mews, first appearing in the Westminster rate books in 1839, is more interesting, with cottages grouped around the central courtyard, and tufts of grass growing between cobbles.

We continue along Lowndes Place and soon behold the oddly free-standing arch of **Belgrave Mews West**. Its isolated position, divorced from the street façade, is surely the result of this listed arch being caught in the middle of the modern Federal German embassy complex, whose architect, unable to demolish it, could not think of a way to incorporate it into his building. Perhaps the forlorn arch sets the pattern for this mews, in which many of the houses have succumbed to indifferent modernizations. **Chesham Mews**, which branches off this mews, has a little more character, but its inhabitants must look out on the far from mews-like Federal Germany embassy building, and must sometimes endure the hum of its roof-top machinery. No 28, boasting two bedrooms and a 'garage-cum-dining room' was going for £115,000 during our visit. The mews gets its name from the home of the Lowndes family in Chesham, Buckinghamshire.

Retracing our steps through the arch now, we proceed to the more

The forlorn, free-standing arch of Belgrave Mews West.

Old Barrack Yard.

conventionally integrated arch of **Belgrave Mews South**, built in about 1830. This is a bright mews, accented by the white mansions outside, and containing a variety of altered cottages. In No 32, the pair of original doors to the former coach-house and stable now lead to a garage which, by itself and without the house, was being offered on a short lease for an amount which would make the average motorist blanch. The dead-end of the mews must have provided a better backdrop before the stable doors of the end house gave way to the two modern overhead garage doors.

Continuing across Eaton Place, we come to **Eccleston Mews**, a cul-de-sac whose first two cottages turn the inside corners of the mews to join with the arch. The Belgian embassy occupies the first few cottages on the southern side, but the southern row is very much disfigured by one of the worst modernizations we have seen; a developer, who unfortunately lacked Cubitt's sense of style, has combined two mews houses into one and turned them into a single 'luxury' house, for which he was asking an astronomical sum for the comparatively short lease of thirty-four years. (The fact that so many of the houses here are still on leaseholds means that the Grosvenors have held on to their leasehold system to this day.) A more refreshing sight was the VCC 1907 Dedion Bouton parked near the dead-end. It looked the proper vintage for a mews.

We continue on Belgrave Place, turning right twice until we reach Wilton Street leading to **Wilton Mews**. Only a patch of cobbling remains in this nicely situated mews with a view of St Peter's Church tower. The mews, which was named for the Earl of Wilton, a Grosvenor, appeared in the Post Office Directory of 1844 with one commercial resident, a builder. The aptly named **Groom Place**, called Chapel Mews until 1931, which we now enter, seems to have been a busier place, with five entries in the Post Office Directory of 1838. It is still a busy place, with the Horse and Groom Tavern in the crook of its right-angle bend, and one of today's rare mews general stores, more often seen in early photographs.

Emerging from Groom Place, we cross diagonally into **Montrose Place** which today has only a few mews cottages left, although its name until 1932, Belgrave Mews East, reveals its original character. The 1844 Post Office Directory lists thirteen residents for this mews, among them a plumber, a glazier, a tailor, a shoemaker, a veterinary surgeon, a beer retailer and the Coachman's Arms. Perhaps the present Old English Coffee House is a small compensation for the disappearance of the former pub. Emerging from Montrose Place, it may be worthwhile having a quick look at the splendid red brick arch with pedestrian entrances to **Headfort Place**, known as Pembroke Mews until 1931. The arch was added to this mews in about 1880, but long before, in 1844, the tavern known as the Triumphal Chariot was listed in the Directory of that year. According to a *Country Life* article of May 1923, the Triumphal Chariot 'started life in Georgian days, enjoyed Victorian prosperity, and then fell into a poor estate, standing untenanted and forlorn, hidden in Pembroke Mews'. It was eventually converted into a private residence.

Walking back towards Belgrave Square, we reach the unpromising entrance to **Wilton Row**. Glancing across the road, we note an arched wooden door, now permanently closed. This leads to **Belgrave Mews North**, a short mews open from Wilton Crescent on the other side. The lower level of this mews gives the arched door the odd appearance, from the mews side, of being suspended in mid-air, without steps leading to it or a reason for its existence. We must leave Belgrave Mews North unseen, however, and proceed along the bends of Wilton Row. This was known as Wilton Crescent Mews until 1937, under which name it appeared in the Westminster rate books by 1832.

Thus we reach the large courtyard which demonstrates the grand scale on which these Grosvenor stables were built. The centre house is said to be occupied by an American film producer who, perhaps in keeping with his profession, has added the theatrical roof and door pediments. This is certainly an equine palace, resembling in size those of the Grosvenor Mayfair estate. No 20, taller than ordinary mews houses, served as a granary. Emerging from the courtyard, we soon come upon the Grenadier, a pub which once served as officers' mess for the Duke of Wellington. It even has its own ghost, which is said to haunt the Grenadier every September in the guise of an officer flogged to death accidentally after cheating at cards.

We continue to the end of the row to look at the interestingly curved end house, overshadowed by the spire of St Paul's Church. Again, the combination of church-yard wall and overhanging trees give this end of the mews a very rural appearance, contrasting oddly with the Bentleys, Mercedes and BMWs we saw parked here. Returning to the Grenadier, we enter the passage next to it, leading to the **Old Barrack Yard**, formerly Percy Cottages. This used to be the stabling yard for the grenadiers. The circular iron staircase with its scalloped cuts-outs exists also in other balconied mews, and the hidden character of this stable yard adds charm to its trim houses. The Grosvenor Estate still reserves some of the cottages here (behind the Grenadier) for old servants of the estate. This gesture is much appreciated by the local tenants, who consider the estate a good landlord. This may well be so today, but in 1888 Frank Banfield was able to observe that 'as far as complaints of hardness and arbitrariness against ground landlords go, they are . . . most on the Grosvenor estate'.

We find the final mews of our Belgravia walk to the right behind the Old Barrack Yard. **Grosvenor Crescent Mews** is perhaps one of the few allowing us to savour the hustle and bustle of the horse days. The mews, which first appeared in Westminster rate books in 1841, contains one of the few working stables left in London, and horses, riders and grooms are constantly coming and going. The insides of the stables, usually open, recall the cramped quarters of former days and the comment of W. J. Gordon in his *The Horse World of London* (1893): 'The stabling in a London mews has not the best of reputations, and its accommodation compares unfavourably with that obtainable at a country town; in fact, it is owing in a great measure to the stable difficulty that so many people job their horses during the London season.'

Aside from the Riding School with its throngs of children in riding costumes, there are some large mews houses with cross-brick patterns. The south-leading arm contains some unrestored houses, one with hoisting beam. Here, within a short distance of Hyde Park Corner, we must leave the tired mews explorer with the consolation that he has taken the final walk of this book.

Stabling in Grosvenor Crescent Mews.

Mayfair

A grander style of cottage often found in Mayfair. This one is in Hays Mews.

ALL the mews areas we have discussed so far have been of nineteenth-century origin and 'suburban' in the sense that they were built during London's great expansion from the city centre to what were then considered the western suburbs. The mews in our final two areas differ greatly from the preceding ones; they were developed in the eighteenth century and they are in more central areas of London.

Being of eighteenth-century origin, they might have been expected to exhibit an older style of architecture and mews building, but there are unfortunately very few examples of genuine eighteenth-century mews left. Many of them were rebuilt under what the *Survey* calls the 'colossal building programme' executed by the first Duke of Westminster during his thirty-year reign (1869–99), which affected many mews including Adam's Row, Balfour Mews and Mount Row.

Being central has meant that the commercial pressure to absorb these mews blocks has been very difficult to resist. Almost all of them have now been paved and lost at least one row of mews cottages. Many remaining houses have been altered almost beyond recognition. For that reason we have picked out only a few of the more interesting mews and individual houses in these areas for discussion. A walk here is suggested only to the most dedicated mews explorer or to one interested in seeing for himself the differences between the typical mews cottage as we have encountered it so often, and these rather grander and less typically mews-like houses.

Mayfair received its present name from the fair which was held there annually, in the first part of the eighteenth century, for fifteen days following 1st May. The fair, which was resented, but nevertheless frequented, by all the nobility in town offered such varied amusements as fire-eating, ass-racing, sausage tables, bull-baiting, grinning for a hat, hasty-pudding eaters, eel-divers and marriages arranged upon one minute's notice.

Undeterred by these noisy goings-on in the south (on the site of the present Shepherd Market), the Grosvenors, as we have already seen, calmly proceeded to lay out their grand estate to the north of the May Fair, giving birth to the original idea of a long mews block set in between the primary and secondary streets which it served. Around Grosvenor Square we find Rex Place, Three Kings Yard, Adam's Row, Lees Place and Davies Mews, for example, many of which are already shown (with their original names) in Roque's *Survey* of 1746.

Knowing of the success the Grosvenors have always had in attracting people of wealth and fashion to their estates, it comes as somewhat of a surprise to learn that no fewer than thirty-eight builders on the Mayfair estate suffered bankruptcy, nine of them between the years 1740 and 1742.

We have earlier quoted Banfield, ever a harsh critic of the great landlords and especially of the Grosvenors, on the injustices of the leasehold system as viewed by an intelligent (though simplistic) child. He adds to this that he 'likes fine streets as much as anyone, but I object to see numbers of Englishmen forced to tax their capital so heavily and perilously merely to suit the dictatorial architectural caprices of a millionaire duke'.

It goes without saying that things were not as black and white as they were painted by Banfield. The question of estate policy, both in regard to architecture and financial gain, is a complex one. The policy varied from estate to estate, and within each estate depended heavily on the particular landlord at the head of the estate. According to the *Survey*, the Grosvenors exercised little control in restricting commercial enterprises, for example, in late eighteenth-century Mayfair. Some attempt was made in early building agreements to restrict taverns and coffeehouses to mews and minor streets, but they were soon to be found in most parts of the estate, along with many other tradesmen.

This attitude contrasts sharply with estate policy a hundred years later.

Above : The May Fair in 1716.
Below : A May Fair notice.

THIS IS TO GIVE NOTICE to all Gentlemen, Ladies and Others, that coming into MAY FAIR, the first Booth on the Left Hand. over against Mr. PINCKETHMAN's Booth, during the usual Time of the Fair, is to be seen, a Great Collection of

Strange and Wonderful Rarities, all Alive,

From several Parts of the World.

A LITTLE BLACK MAN, lately brought from the *West Indies*, being the Wonder of the Age, he being but 3 foot high, and 25 years old. .

Likewise, TWO WOOD MONSTERS, from the *East Indies*, Male and Female, being the Admirablest Creatures that ever was seen in this Kingdom : they differ from all *Creatures* whatsoever ; and are so Wonderful in Nature, that it is too large to insert here.

Also, a Little MARMOSET, from the *East Indies*, which by a great deal of Pains, is now brought to that Perfection, that no Creature of his Kind, ever perform'd the like : he exercises by the Word of Command ; he Dances the *Chesshire-rounds* ; he also Dances with Two Naked Swords, and performs several other Pretty Fancies. Likewise, a Noble CIVET CAT from *Guiny*, which is admir'd for his Beauty, and that incomparable Scent which perfumes the whole Place. Also, a MUNTOSH from *Rushy*, being very wonderfully marked.

Also, a HELLISCOPE from *Argier*, being the Beautifuls Creature in all the World ; specked like a *Leopard*.

VIVAT REGINA.

Among the innumerable trades a tenant in Brook's Mews, cited by the *Survey*, undertook not to practise, were that of 'butcher, fishmonger, slaughterer, horse boiler, cat gut spinner, cart grease maker, soap boiler, sugar baker, dyer, scourer, alehouse keeper, licensed victualler, blacksmith, undertaker, gold-beater, bone boiler, corn burner, chimney sweeper, dealer in soot, dealer in second-hand clothes, or any other trade, business or employment which shall be dangerous or a nuisance or annoyance to the adjoining tenants and occupiers'.

This long list contains many of the very trades early Post Office Directories show mews dwellers as practising, so policy often fluctuated, and was also not always strictly enforced, notwithstanding Banfield's many tales of businesses and professions ruined by Grosvenor interference. Banfield relates how butchers in Mount Street, for example, were compelled by the Duke to sign away the right to hang carcasses outside their shop-windows on a rail. A butcher remarked feelingly on the subject: 'A row of clean, white carcasses is rather a taking and pretty object'; and Banfield adds that 'Mount Street would, perhaps, have been none the worse if the monotony of the southern façade had been broken by the raw material of the roast beef of Old England swaying in the breeze'. In the days before refrigeration, one cannot help but sympathize with the Grosvenors on this point. Nor can we be too upset with the estate when it prohibited one Colonel Augustus Meyrick in 1865 to keep a cow, in spite of his lawyer's opinion that 'some gentlemen like to keep a cow in London'.

The Grosvenors' attitude toward the architecture of their estate also varied with each particular duke (or perhaps with the amount of time each duke spent in the south of France, delegating his affairs to one of his agents). In general they chose the architects for the building and re-building on their estate themselves, and laid down the overall policies. Such choices were not always made strictly on merit, as when Eustace Balfour, brother of the future prime minister and nephew by marriage of the Duke of Westminster himself, became the estate surveyor and a prolific builder of private houses on the estate (incidentally giving his name to Balfour Mews). The dukes themselves had widely differing tastes, often reflecting the fashion of the time, and while one of them, for example, liked and required the Italianate stucco so prevalent in the mid-nineteenth century, his successor supported the Queen Anne revival and was a 'fervent admirer of the new South Kensington red brick and terracotta manner'. One of the dukes' liking for plate glass windows went against the architectural taste of his surveyor, and his fondness for occasionally painting stucco work orange recalls Banfield's complaint about the architectural caprices of millionaire dukes.

On the question of financial gain, where Banfield casts the Grosvenors and the rest of the landlords so rigidly into the mould of the ruthlessly money-hungry Shylocks, the judgement of Balfour's wife was perhaps more balanced. She thought that the estate 'was run, not as today on commercial lines, but more as a Principality'. The estate was thus subject to the whims of the governing duke, rather than to the mechanics of profit and loss. In spite of Banfield's statements to the contrary, the *Survey* reports that the duke's lessees had reasons to be satisfied, for they 'invariably got their money back'.

Though the Dukes were arbitrary and often kept their tenants on tenterhooks as to whether they would be allowed to renew their leases and how high a premium they were to pay for this privilege, they also went out of their way to see that conditions in the poorer areas were kept up to certain standards. Under Eustace Balfour, a typical requirement of the estate was to 'modernize the stabling as regards accommodation for a married coachman and one helper, providing at least four rooms (every room to have a fireplace) and a separate W.C. for the use of the helpers. The helper's room to be approached directly from the staircase, and to be kept quite distinct from the coachman's quarters.'

In 1887, the Duke's agent Boodle (who frequently draws Banfield's greatest scorn) stated before a Select Committee of the House of Commons that the Duke's aim was to have 'wide thoroughfares instead of narrow, to set back the houses in rebuilding so as to obtain broad areas and a good basement for the servants . . . He also wished to have effective architecture, to insist upon good sanitary arrangements in houses, to promote . . . schools and open spaces for recreation . . . and that he likes a handsome town, and would sacrifice enormously to carry that out on his estate.' According to the *Survey*, the Duke of Westminster did sacrifice a very considerable extra income by rebuilding and improving the estate, perhaps as much as two-thirds of what he could have obtained. It must also be noted that the ground rents, which Banfield calls 'heavy', are, by today's standards quite modest, and that the profit from selling a lease nowadays goes to the tenant rather than the landlord.

The outbreak of World War I interrupted the rebuilding programme by the Grosvenors's then current architect, Edmund Wimperis. Wimperis quickly realized that the war had 'revolutionized the circumstances dealing with property' and noted the success of a tenant who had 'converted stabling in Aldford Street into a little house making it the best bijou house in London'. Convinced that there would now be a great demand for this type of thing, Wimperis in the 1920s rebuilt several decrepit small houses and stables in Culross Street. According to the *Survey*, the age of the mews house in a fashionable district had arrived.

The outbreak of World War I also marked a fundamental change in the social character of the estate, according to the *Survey*. Thereafter, the number of private residents kept steadily falling, and offices and businesses, so often strenuously kept out before, gradually invaded the estate. Cocktail parties, cabarets and intimate night clubs replaced the lavish receptions of Edwardian times, and it became fashionable in Mayfair to pretend poverty, perhaps another reason for the success of the bijou mews house. Let us now look at a few of the remaining mews and bijou houses to see how they compare with what we have seen previously.

The ornate gables and ventilation turrets of Adam's Row.

Adam's Row Called Adam's Mews until 1937, it already appeared in Roque's *Survey* under that name. The northern row of the mews gave way to the modern Britannia Hotel, whose architect made no attempt to integrate its style with that of the splendid southern row. This row contains mews houses of the grander type, with hoisting beams, upper-storey external doors, ornate gables, and attractive ventilating turrets. According to the *Survey*, Adam's Row, along with Reeves, Balfour and other Mayfair mews, housed many of the Grosvenor Estate residents displaced by the business and office invasion of the estate.

Balfour Mews Many of the houses here, like the southern row of Adam's Row, date from the last quarter of the nineteenth century, when these mews were part of the great rebuilding programme under the reign of the first Duke of Westminster. Like vintage wines of certain regions, Mayfair mews houses which date from these years always conform to very high standards. Eustace Balfour, the Grosvenor architect who gave his name to the mews, certainly participated in the rebuilding of it in the years 1898–9. According to the *Survey*, the stables on the east side of Balfour Mews show late Queen Anne elevations at their best, with 'delightfully shaped gables and individual touches of Arts and Crafts detailing and carving upon each house'.

MEWS AREAS IN MAYFAIR

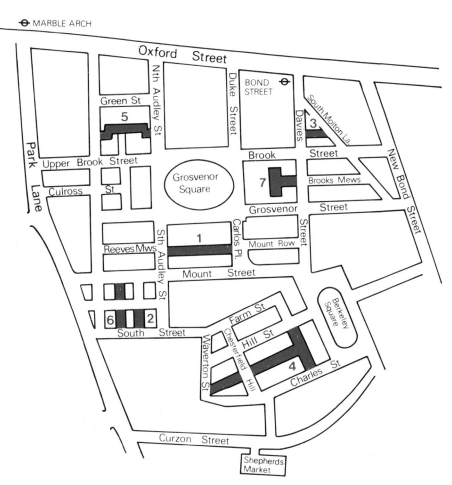

1 Adam's Row
2 Balfour Mews
3 Davies Mews
4 Hays Mews
5 Lees Place
6 Rex Place
7 Three Kings Yard

Davies Mews So named for poor little rich Mary Davies, whom we met earlier. (Although she was declared insane, she has the dubious compensation of having a London Street and mews named after her.) The Mews was near the site of Grosvenor market, established in the 1780s which, being somewhat out of the way, was not a great success. In the latter part of the nineteenth century, tenants in the front houses often complained of the 'uproarious conduct' of the children at the Ragged School in Davies Mews. Today the north side of the mews is occupied by Gray's Antique Market in the Mews, who have added ornately fake details to the façade of their building.

Hays Mews This mews (part of the Berkeley Estate), though wider than most and paved, is among the most interesting of the remaining mews in Mayfair. No 26, shown on page 118 in an old photograph, has changed little over the years, nor have Nos 28 and 29, one of which has a dormer gable. There are (for Mayfair) unusually small cottages like No 17, and equine palaces like Nos 4, 40 and 41. Here we also find what must be one of the last remaining pissoirs in London. The first Duke of Westminster had been 'most anxious for a great many more urinals (*à la mode française*) being erected in the Parish and in London generally'. When one of the coachmen complained that the urinal in Reeves Mews 'could be seen into from his upper windows' the governing board acted promptly to alleviate this offending circumstance. The mews, built in about 1750, betrays its rural origin by its name.

Lees Place Called Lees Mews until 1930, the name refers to a Mr Robert Lee or Lees, a victualler, who was the first proprietor of a tavern which stood at the entrance to the mews. No 3 Lees Place, a substantial mews house even by Mayfair standards, was built by the noted architect J. T. Wimperis in 1889, and converted in modern times by H. Douglas Kidd, who rather spoiled Wimperis's Victorian roof-line.

Rex Place There are some interesting houses with stepped gables, of the larger type of Mayfair mews house. Known until 1938 as Street's Mews, it then became King's Mews, and finally acquired the Latin word for king in 1951. The identity of the king is unknown.

Three Kings Yard Today this former stable yard is notable mainly for the grand building with clock and arched entrance straddling its end. According to the 1871 census almost all the male working residents here were coachmen and grooms. The only exception were pub-keepers, and they might well have belonged to the Three Kings pub which stood at the entrance of the mews until 1879.

Hays Mews, Mayfair (1924).

An equine palace, Hays Mews.
Below : Three Kings Yard.

Above right : 3 Lees Place before conversion (1890); *Below :* after conversion (1980).

The Manor House, Marylebone, became a school for the children of the gentry in 1703. It was demolished in 1791, when livery stables were built on the site, which later became Devonshire Place Mews.

Marylebone

THIS tongue-twister of a name was taken from the church on the High Street, which was called St Mary-a-le-bourne (St Mary by Tyburn) and replaced the earlier name of Tyburn because of its unsavoury association with the gallows of that name. Henry VIII built himself a hunting lodge here, curiously enough on the site of the later Devonshire Place Mews. The royal presence made the village of St Marylebone into a kind of playground for kings, queens, nobility and their retinues. Their high jinks continued until the time of Oliver Cromwell, when Henry's playground became Marylebone Park. After the Civil War in the seventeenth century, the park reverted to farmland, and the new farmers supplied London with milk, eggs and meat.

For a time St Marylebone was content to remain a small village with its church, manor house and winding lane besides the Tyburn. But the one hour's walking distance from London was not enough to preserve the village's isolation. In the eighteenth century it became a residential estate on the city outskirts, when squares, houses, gardens, trees and statues all appeared in quick succession. Cunningham reports that 'by 1739 there were 577 houses in Marylebone parish and thirty-five persons who kept coaches . . .' These thirty-five persons may have used outside stabling for their horses, but it was only a matter of time before the rapid increase in population would create mews blocks for London's 'newest and most fashionable centre of aristocratic wealth'.

Building north of Oxford Street was begun in 1717 on the estate of Edward Harley, later second Earl of Oxford (thus Harley and Oxford Streets.) In 1812, James Morgan laid out Regent's Park from the plans of John Nash on the site of the former Marylebone Park. It was named for the Prince Regent, popularly known as 'Prinny'. The rest of the Crown Estate was covered with elegant crescents and terraces again designed by that 'unorthodox, slap-dash genius' John Nash, with his good friend Prinny's firm support.

We shall consider mews falling mainly into the areas covered by two of the Marylebone estates—confusingly called Portman and Portland. In 1553 Sir William Portman, Lord Chief Justice of England, bought 270 acres in Marylebone parish. The Portman Estate is bounded very approximately by Oxford Street, Edgware Road, Regent's Park and Marylebone Lane. The other big land-owners in this area, whose estate extended eastwards of Marylebone Lane, were the dukes of Portland, who came into their land when the second Duke married young Lady Margaret Cavendish Harley in 1734.

Henry William Portman began to develop his estate in the mid-eighteenth century, and many of its mews date from the latter half of that century. Both the estates have some of the highest mews densities in London, but this, unfortunately, does not automatically make it an area of great interest to the mews explorer. As in Mayfair, the central position of these mews has subjected them to intense commercial pressure, so that most of them have lost their cobbles and at least one row of mews cottages. As in other central districts, many of the mews here have been so totally absorbed by the city that they are beyond recognition as mews. All the tell-tale signs are gone.

Not so very long ago, the maze of mews in Marylebone (many of which survive only in their street names) could still provide the setting for a Sherlock Holmes adventure:

He gave a most searching glance to right and left, and at every subsequent corner he took the utmost pains to assure that he was not followed. Our route was certainly a singular one. Holmes' knowledge of the by-ways of London was extraordinary and on this occasion he passed rapidly and with an assured step through a network of mews and stables the very existence of which I had never known.

(Watson in 'The Adventure of the Empty House'.)

We have quoted earlier the opinion of Frank Banfield, writing in 1888 on the great landlords of London, in which he found the Grosvenor Estate the harshest with its tenants, and the Portland the most lenient. The Portman fell somewhere in between, but Banfield was particularly concerned with that estate, as in 1888, at the very time he was writing, all the ninety-nine year leases fell in, allowing the landlord 'to draw handsome premiums and raise the ground rent to seven and eightfold their original figure'. The prospect of these riches moved Banfield to exclaim that the 'modern Pactolus, the genuine El Dorado, must be sought by the topographical explorer of today somewhere in the vicinage of Baker Street. We Englishmen,' he continues, 'are not, on the whole, over fond of geography,

An unusual house in Devonshire Row Mews, one of the few Marylebone mews where cobbles remain.

but we do love wealth; we can rise into something like sentiment as we see the big moneybags mounting up, tier after tier, round any favoured mortal.'

What Banfield may not have taken into consideration was that during the ninety-nine years duration of these leases, land in London had certainly increased seven- or eightfold in value. Banfield thought in 1888 that the Portmans would cause Croesus to turn in his grave; Banfield himself, however, would go into a tailspin if he could realize the size of the premiums paid on exchange of leases today. Because the ground rents have not increased dramatically due to long leases (most of the Portman leases renewed in 1888 would still be running today!) all increases, often a thousandfold or more, have gone into the premiums, or sales, of leases. But today the tenants and speculators, especially those clever enough to buy the leases when they are low and sell them when they are high, have been the chief beneficiaries, seeing the money-bags mounting up tier after tier, while the ground landlords are still collecting modest rents, fixed in the dim and distant past.

It is hard today to understand the fury and contempt aroused in many famous people from Dickens to Disraeli, by the architecture of some Marylebone streets, especially in the Harley and Wimpole Streets area. Dickens called Harley Street 'grim', and Disraeli thought it was flat, dull and spiritless, with the streets resembling each other like a large family of plain children. Someone else thought Harley Street was 'cut out of cardboard'. If they thought this of the principal streets, what must they have thought of the many mews near Harley Street, some of which, like Devonshire Close and Weymouth Mews, are today among Marylebone's quietest and most civilized streets?

Though Marylebone today covers too large an area to give it a unified character of its own, or to identify it by a catchy phrase such as 'arty' Chelsea, 'aristocratic' Mayfair, or 'elegant' Belgravia, it did, in the past, evoke much admiration in spite of the harsh critics cited above. We have seen how it progressed from royal pleasure resort and fashionable centre of aristocratic wealth, to its lively Regency and Victorian days, with the theatrical array of grandly conceived villas and terraces. Dickens, one of its harshest critics, lived there himself, and so did Constable, the Brownings, Turner, Dr Johnson, Boswell, George Eliot, Herbert Spencer, and even Wagner during his visits to England.

Gordon Mackenzie thinks it not unlikely that the famous boulevards of Paris may have owed something to Nash. He quotes Taine, a French critic and historian, who was able to write of Marylebone:

> Paris is mediocre in comparison with these crescents, circuses, and the endless rows of monumental houses built of massive stone, with porticos and carved fronts lining very wide streets. There are fifty as wide as the Rue de la Paix. There can be no question that Napoleon III demolished Paris and rebuilt it because he had lived in London [In the St John's Wood area of Marylebone].

It is therefore more in the spirit of the glorious past than the disappointing present that we must approach the remaining mews of interest here.

MEWS AREAS IN MARYLEBONE

1 Cross Keys Close
2 Devonshire Close
3 Devonshire Mews North
4 Gloucester Place Mews
5 Montagu Mews North
6 Montagu Mews South
7 Welbeck Way
8 Weymouth Mews

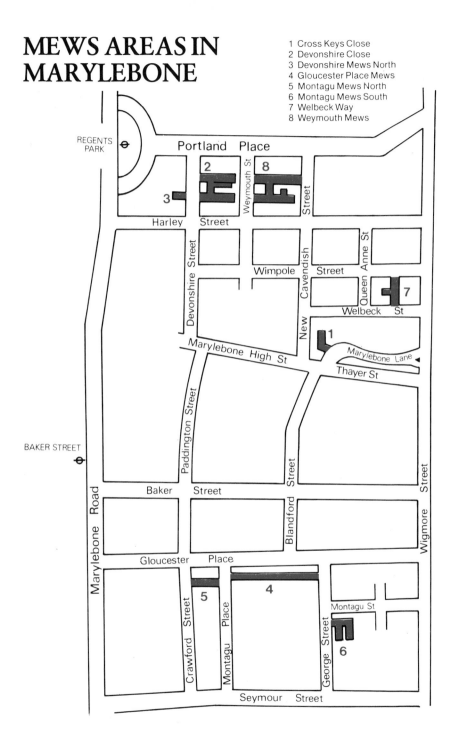

Devonshire Close.

The following mews in Marylebone, arranged alphabetically, are either of some interest in themselves, or contain mews houses of note:

Cross Keys Close This unusual name derives from the inn of that name (now the Prince Alfred) which used to stand at its entrance. Philip Keys, a carpenter, built the mews in the 1770s, and it was first rated in 1785. Now predominantly commercial, it has an unusually narrow passage winding off to the north.

Devonshire Close Called Devonshire Mews East from 1899 to 1934, it had the much more romantic name of Cape of Good Hope Mews before that. There is an interesting mixture here, containing some large brick-faced houses, and this is one of the few central mews still to retain its cobbles. It is an extensive, many-armed mews, containing a number of interesting houses, including some attractive Tudor imitations.

Montagu Mews North.

Devonshire Mews North This small, whitewashed courtyard group is perhaps not typical of this area. It entered the rate books first in 1785, and its connection with Devonshire comes through the Cavendishes, who were also the Earls of Devonshire.

Gloucester Place Mews was named after George III's favourite brother, Prince William, created Duke of Gloucester in 1764; Gloucester Place was built shortly after. It is a long residential mews with many projections, giving it an interesting, somewhat cluttered look.

Montagu Mews North A real surprise awaits us here—well hidden in this mews is a galleried yard reminiscent of De Vere Mews. Montagu Mews, Place, Row and Street were all named for Mrs Elizabeth Montague, who came to live in Marylebone in 1781. Often referred to as the 'original bluestocking' (a woman having or affecting literary tastes—i.e. talking about literature instead of playing cards), she lavishly entertained writers and artists, and every May Day gave a great feast for chimney-sweeps 'so that they might enjoy ONE happy day in the year'.

126

Montagu Mews South.

Montagu Mews South is an F-shaped mews with good cobbles, over-hanging trees and some unaltered houses.

Welbeck Way This was called Little Welbeck Street until 1936, after Welbeck Abbey in Nottinghamshire, which, after the dissolution of the monasteries, came into the hands of the Cavendish family and was part of the dowry of Lady Henrietta Cavendish when she married Edward Harley. Today only the two last houses in its dead-end arm are worth a look.

Weymouth Mews was named for the third Viscount Weymouth who married Lady Elizabeth Cavendish, an 'agreeable, engaging creature' made much more agreeable and engaging by virtue of her brother's Marylebone estate. Weymouth himself undertook to build houses on his estate—an unusual practice for the ground landlords—and named street and mews after himself in the process. This many-armed mews is as interesting and extensive as the nearby Devonshire Close. It is especially noted for its pretty pub, the Dover Castle.

Above : Welbeck Way.
Right : The Dover Castle public house in Weymouth Mews.

The Mews
in Modern
London

W E have now looked at a great variety of mews and can begin to consider their character as it emerges from our scrutiny. It can safely be said that the mews are a highly unusual environment for a modern city.* We have seen in our historical discussion how the mews, as adjuncts to the residences of the upper classes, came to be situated in prime areas of London. Unlike the houses they served, which were mostly located on principal streets and thus in the public eye and in the path of traffic, the mews managed to escape notice and congestion alike. They were left to fend for themselves, benignly neglected by history.

The mews' unusual position—central, yet out of the way—is undoubtedly one of the factors which has made them highly prized in the house market. It is, in fact, not unreasonable to suggest the new construction of mews-like streets where historical accident has not provided them. Modern city builders could profitably copy the essentials of a mews street; the privacy, the hidden character, the lack of traffic, the individuality, the (until recently) easy-to-afford smallness of the houses, the lower cost of rates and maintenance, the close proximity to work and shopping, the sense of community, the pride of ownership and the feeling of country village in city centre. But to achieve this, the modern builders must not construct artificial closes with artificially created curves, containing houses so alike that their owners have trouble distinguishing their own front door at night. Superficially mews-like, this would be a dreary suburban-like neighbourhood which dulls the senses and forces its younger inhabitants to flee it or destroy it by acts of vandalism.

To make such a building scheme successful, house buyers, like mews dwellers, would have to be allowed to exercise their imagination on their houses and finish them off both inside and out to suit their individual tastes. Perhaps the builders could provide only the essential structures, or semi-derelict houses in central areas could be sold for a few hundred pounds to people who pledge to restore them.

Any modern re-creation of mews might also try to eliminate their disadvantages. Popular as mews houses are, they do have many disadvantages, mostly arising from the fact that they were not principally built to be lived in, and that they were built by a society which thought less of their grooms than their horses. Many mews houses are too small. (The spiral staircase of one mews house is too narrow for any piece of furniture larger than a chair to be moved. This house has a kitchen $6\frac{1}{2}' \times 9'$, a living room $10' \times 10'$, and a single bedroom $7\frac{1}{2}' \times 10'$, plus a very small garage.)†

*A somewhat comparable phenomenon developed in Washington with the construction of some 250 alleys, containing 3500 two-storey houses, by speculative builders in the nineteenth century. They were built to satisfy the demand for cheap housing, and constituted 'a world of their own', inhabited mainly by poor blacks. But unlike the mews, of which a great number survive, there are only about twenty inhabited alleys left in Washington.

†Critics of mews houses frequently call them 'pokey'. Many of them are small, but we have seen many truly substantial ones on our walks. Many look deceptively small from the outside. Here is the description of an average-looking mews cottage in the Paddington area: Ground Floor: entrance hall and integral garage $20' \times 7\frac{1}{2}'$; living and dining area $37\frac{1}{4}' \times 17\frac{1}{2}'$; rear bedroom $17' \times 14\frac{1}{4}'$ (with domed glass skylight); kitchen $11' \times 10'$; bath. First Floor: 2nd bedroom $14\frac{3}{4}' \times 13\frac{3}{4}'$; 3rd bedroom $15\frac{3}{4}' \times 7\frac{1}{4}'$; 4th bedroom $18\frac{1}{4}' \times 11'$; 2nd bathroom.

Children playing in a London mews.

The lack of rear or side windows means not only a want of light and cross-ventilation, but a tendency to be exposed to the scrutiny of one's neighbours. In order to have adequate light, the front windows must be kept clear of blinds or curtains, but the narrowness of most mews streets allows a commanding view of the opposite cottage. We have observed some mews houses whose blinds are practically never raised.

Notwithstanding their quiet position, mews do have a noise problem at times, as any sounds originating there tend to echo throughout them. Cars in cul-de-sac mews starting early in the morning and awkwardly trying to negotiate a U-turn are usually more effective than alarm clocks in rousing the remaining sleepers. Parties or radios late at night are similarly disturbing. A mews dweller sitting in front of his house and hearing the telephone ring may dash in to answer it only to discover that it was his neighbour's. He may have been sitting in front of his house to take the air or get some sun, since he seldom has a garden or yard for that purpose.

But the advantages of the mews, as we have already enumerated them for the attention of modern city builders, far outweigh their drawbacks. The long list of the mews' virtues can be extended still further: children can play here undisturbed by the occasional traffic; people often prefer the rare chance to own a small house in the city to the more usual flat; and the mews-dwellers' frequent surveillance of their short and narrow blocks

THE MEWS IN MODERN LONDON

from low windows (especially at the slightest sign of activity) makes these houses more difficult to burgle or vandalize than the larger, more impersonal front houses—an important advantage considering the increasing violence in the modern city.

Aside from the benign neglect of history which we mentioned earlier, the mews in modern London have survived because people choose to live there. In this, they are at odds with city planners, who seem to show a remarkable lack of interest in where and how city dwellers want to live. One of the first of these planners, Sir Patrick Geddes (a disciple of Ebenezer Howard, famous for his idea of the 'Garden City'), sets the pattern for the planners who follow him, in his book *Cities in Evolution* (1915). After expressing the opinion that the mews are rapidly becoming obsolete, he warns that 'now is the very time for city improvers'. Since the 'hygienist has fully demonstrated the unwholesomeness of mews', he suggests that the city use some of them for garages and workshops, but that 'large demolitions of them would also be possible, with not inconsiderable gain to the needed open spaces'.

There is not a word here about housing people in the mews, even though at the very time Geddes was writing, the bijou house began to be popular in the Mayfair mews. The 'open spaces' mentioned here are always dearer to the planners' hearts than living spaces for people. We have seen these open spaces around modern developments, windswept and desolate, and unfrequented by the people for whom they were designed. We can look at the site of Polygon Mews and the north side of Chilworth and Eastbourne Mews to see what open spaces accomplished there. Geddes, like most city planners who follow him, distrusts people's capacity to make decisions about their city, and wants to bring in the 'city improvers'. Olsen makes the interesting point that unlike the promoters of the West End estates in London, who gave the customer what he wanted, the twentieth-century town planner is more of a moral reformer who wants to remake the customer. In doing so, he condemns his client to live in places he himself would be most unlikely to reside in. (A modern architect with a sense of humour has suggested a survey to see how many of his colleagues live in their own creations rather than in period houses.)

The threat to the mews in modern times comes from two sources, one obvious and the other more subtle. The obvious threat is the constant danger of demolition or redevelopment which hangs not only over the mews but every city street. Already at the end of the nineteenth century, the Bedford Estate had pulled down a large number of mews to make room for progress in the shape of London University, hotels, garages and roads. Abbey, Tavistock and Woburn Mews were pulled down in 1897, Southampton Mews disappeared in 1898, Keppel Mews North and South, and Torrington Mews bit the dust in 1901, to be followed by Russell Mews in 1905–6 and Charlotte Mews in 1910. Many more fell victim to the developers' fever which gripped London in the 1950s, '60s and early '70s (perhaps an up-to-date version of the Great Plague and the Great Fire

Tavistock Mews photographed in 1895; it was demolished in 1897.   133

combined?) which was so well documented in Christopher Booker's *Good-Bye London* and the subsequent BBC programme *City of Towers*. These decades saw the demise or total disfigurement of Redfield Lane, and Hippodrome, Jay, Ashburn, Bott's and Stephen Mews among many others.

At present the threat from redevelopment has somewhat receded, as many mews are located within conservation areas, and the Greater London Council and the London Boroughs are much more cautious about allowing new developments. A case in point is a group of mews cottages in Alba Place, off Portobello Road which the Royal Borough of Kensington and Chelsea call an 'opportunity site'. In their *Planning News* for January and February 1980, the cottages are referred to as 'dilapidated mews properties', having 'no aesthetic merit whatever', and requiring redevelopment as the 'only possible means of improvement'. In spite of this possibly harsh judgement, Kensington themselves refused the builder's redevelopment plans as being 'contrary to Council policy'. The reasons given show that Kensington Council has come a long way from the days of Sir Patrick Geddes and his followers. The council would like to keep these cottages as storage spaces for street traders of the nearby antique market, thus retaining the character and function of the neighbourhood.

The developers have now come back with a new proposal which respects the Council's wishes. Under this plan, they would keep the ground-level former stables for the traders, and add two floors of flats above them, using matching red brick, timber sash windows and wooden doors. Best of all, they envisage the construction of an arch at the mews entrance, incorporating additional accommodation in the arch itself. (Perhaps the first instance of a modern mews arch!) These are encouraging signs that some of the people who now make our planning decisions have begun to absorb the lessons so clearly spelled out in Jane Jacobs' work *The Death and Life of Great American Cities* (1961).

Here the author takes a close look at the delicate and intricate mechanism of existing and working cities, rather than the utopias envisaged by most planners. Among the many ideas which apply to London, Miss Jacobs discusses what she calls 'unslumming', which is basically the process by which houses and neighbourhoods regenerate themselves (if left alone by the authorities) simply because they are desirable places to live in. Houses in such areas eventually fall into the hands of people who cherish them and lovingly repair or restore them. We have observed the process in Bathurst Mews (which the Hyde Park Estate in 1972 called 'wholly unsatisfactory'), but it can be seen all over London's West End, particularly around Westbourne and Ladbroke Groves, and lately even in parts of London's East End.

The propensity of our modern planners to shy away from what Geddes dismisses as 'modest tackings on, patchings, and cobblings' and to sweep away the past, throwing out the baby with the bathwater, is not new. The Georgians managed to find fault with Tudor and Stuart architecture and

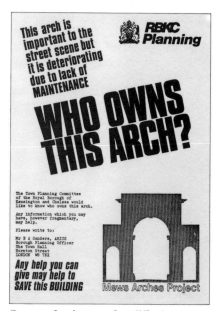

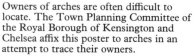

Owners of arches are often difficult to locate. The Town Planning Committee of the Royal Borough of Kensington and Chelsea affix this poster to arches in an attempt to trace their owners.

This mews house has been modernized beyond recognition.

Alba Place in 1980; plans for redevelopment were refused.

did their best to destroy what remained of it after the Great Fire. Olsen shows very clearly that the Victorians had a passionate dislike of anything Georgian, and our modern mania for destroying old buildings of all periods shows that we have learned little from the experience of our predecessors. Indeed, one purpose of this book is to contribute to the awareness that the architecture of the past can not only make a viable, but a preferred environment for living, because of its emphasis on the human scale and the human individual in its designs. The very 'tackings on, patchings, and cobblings' so despised by Geddes are probably the way a

Henniker Mews—a traffic-free oasis.

city can best grow organically; it is the way to keep good old buildings, age-old street patterns and the character of neighbourhoods intact without destroying the fabric of the past.

The image of nineteenth-century London with its fog, grime, child-labour, slums and ragged schools may have blinded us to its splendid architectural heritage. 'London rarely attempts to look like a great city, being content to be one,' Olsen wrote. He points out that the Victorian legacy has left us an astoundingly diverse style of architecture, a *mélange* which would detract from the grandeur and unity of a city like Paris with

its boulevards and monuments, but which shows the tremendous freedom, individuality and vitality possessed by the builders of Victorian London.

The other more subtle threat to the mews is ironically due to their very success as places to live. Jane Jacobs shows that the popularity of a neighbourhood will soon attract so many people who wish to live there, that all but those who can pay the most are eliminated. 'These are usually childless people,' she writes, 'and today they are not simply people who can pay the most in general, but people who can or will pay the most for the smallest space . . . Families are crowded out, variety of scene is crowded out . . .' The very charm admired in the first place 'is destroyed by its . . . new occupants, by the act of occupation'. In the mews, we find numerous examples of this process when the houses become impossibly 'twee' or are modernized in such poor taste as to leave little of the original charm. The variety supplied by families with children, and light commercial use, disappears with the uniformity of the new occupants, and their ability, being well off, to make drastic and often unfortunate alterations.

The problem of preventing excesses of bad taste by individual builders or restorers without imposing rigid and uniform architectural styles dictated from above (by governing authorities) is hardly new. The *Building News* in 1873 thought that the rebuilding of London demonstrated the superiority of British individualism over the conformity imposed by the state on the rebuilding of Paris. 'No Imperial edict has decreed in our case the demolition of the city which existed in order to rebuild one of theoretical perfection . . . All that has been done here has been done by private enterprise and in a prudential spirit . . .' The *Building News* preferred the London method: '. . . we would rather stand the risk of being occasionally shocked, than lose the chance of being sometimes, though less frequently, charmed.' The merit of the mews of London is that we are more frequently charmed than shocked.

In addition to these two major threats to the continued existence and preservation of the mews, a minor threat to only the mews arches arises from the curious fact that the owners of the arches are often difficult to locate, and thus no one can be found who will assume responsibility for their maintenance. The leaflet reproduced on page 135 issued by the Kensington Council, is sometimes attached to a mews arch. As we have seen, these arches were often built by nineteenth-century developers to screen the mews and enhance the principal streets, a device first thought of by John Nash in his development around Regent's Park. Although all the houses in a given estate were covered by leases, no one seems to have bothered to issue a legal document on the mews arch. Since most of the estates have gone through many changes, it now becomes difficult if not impossible to sort out which arches belong to whom. A report by the Kensington Town Planning Committee in April 1978 cited a survey among mews dwellers on the popularity of their arches. Only a single person in this poll expressed the view that if demolished, they would soon be forgotten.

The arched entrance to Redcliffe Mews (1971).

In her introduction to *The Origin of Street Names*, Gillian Bebbington points out how the 'pig-headedness of landowners [in the sixteenth century] is strikingly visible on the map of Mayfair . . .' She shows how estate owners planned and built only for their own estate, and that there is an almost total lack of communication (for example) between Grosvenor and Berkeley lands. 'London,' she continues, 'is a maze of pointless cul-de-sacs, winding lanes, streets at an oblique angle to the main road, and streets with kinks in the middle, which far outnumber the direct routes from A to B. Such has been the course of English history, that London never had the chance of other world cities, such as New York, Moscow, or even Paris, of forming on a logical grid. Its irrational development is the result of property divisions dating in many cases from Tudor times.'

We would like to make the point that London's 'maze of pointless cul-de-sacs and winding lanes' is also London's great strength. Let us compare the experience of a shopper using New York's 'logical, economical grid' with the same shopper in London's winding lanes and cul-de-sacs. We will take two examples of comparative stores and locations, Macy's on 34th Street coupled with Selfridges on Oxford Street, and Bloomingdale's on Third Avenue coupled with Harrods in Knightsbridge. After being jostled by shopping crowds in both cities, and having exhausted both cash and patience, the New York shopper emerges from Macy's or Bloomingdale's to confront more crowds, honking automobiles, traffic lights and the unrelenting pace of the city, no matter from which exit he emerges. The shop windows and throngs of people so exciting on his way to the store, now become tiresome and wearying. The logical economic street grid has made certain that every single street in it is a through street, holding as much traffic as it can bear. It has made certain that the east to west blocks in the grid system are uniformly long without the relief of criss-crossing shortcuts.

The same shopper emerging from Selfridges or Harrods is in a more fortunate position. He can soon escape the crowds of Oxford Street or Knightsbridge by choosing one of the store's back exits and ducking into quiet alleys, mews and squares not far from either store. He can criss-cross through a maze of streets, avoiding shoppers and traffic. The crowds of people and cars avoid these lanes because they have no reason to use them, because they will not lead anywhere in particular, because they are, in fact, 'pointless'.

The countless backwaters and traffic-free oases, which history has so freely bestowed on us, are refreshing to visitor and inhabitant alike. They contribute greatly toward making London one of the world's most civilized cities. Whether by accident or design, the understatement of these quiet, hidden places, containing within them so much that is individual, are expressive of the English character. We would like to think that the mews of London reflect this and are central to the history and traditions of London.

Bibliography

Banfield, Frank *The Great Landlords of London.* S. Blackett, 1890.

Bebbington, Gillian *London Street Names.* Batsford, 1972.

Birch, John *Examples of Stables.* W. Blackwood & Sons, 1892.

Booker, Christopher and Candida L. Green *Good-Bye London.* Fontana, 1973.

Booth, Charles *Life and Labour of the People in London.* Macmillan & Co., 1902.

Borer, Mary Cathcart *Two Villages—The Story of Chelsea and Kensington.* W. H. Allen, 1973.

Borer, Mary Cathcart *The Years of Grandeur.* W. H. Allen, 1976.

Clinch, George *Marylebone and St Pancras.* Truslove & Shirley, 1890.

Clunn, Harold P. *The Face of London.* Phoenix House Ltd, 1951.

Coleman, T. E. *Stable Sanitation and Construction.* E. & F. N. Spon, 1897.

Cook, E. T. *Highways and Byways in London.* MacMillan & Co., 1903.

Creswell, H. B. 'Seventy Years Back', *Architectural Review*, December 1958.

Dyos, H. J. and Michael Wolf (Ed) *Victorian City: Images and Realities.* Vol I. Routledge & Kegan Paul, 1973.

Fitzwygram, Sir F. W. J. *Horses and Stables.* Longman & Co., 1894.

Geddes, Sir Patrick *Cities in Evolution.* Ernest Benn Ltd, 1915.

Giraud, Byng *Stable Building and Stable Fitting.* Batsford, 1891.

Girouard, Mark 'Sacrifice to the Ladies', *Country Life*, January 29, 1959, pp. 198–99.

Gladstone, Florence *Notting Hill in Bygone Days.* T. Fisher Unwin, Ltd, 1924.

Gordon, W. J. *The Horse World of London.* The Leisure Hour Library, 1893.

Hare, Augustus *Walks in London.* Vol 2, George Allen, 1901.

Hillier, T. 'On the Mortality in Mews', *Transactions of the National Association for the Promotion of Social Sciences*, 1859, pp. 569–570.

Hollingshead, J. *Ragged London in 1861.* Smith, Elder & Co. 1861.

Huggett, Frank *Carriages at Eight.* Lutterworth Press, 1979.

Hunt, Leigh *The Old Court Suburb.* Hurst & Blackett, 1855.

The Hyde Park Estate Report prepared for the Church Commissioners, August 1972.

Jacobs, Jane *The Death and Life of Great American Cities.* Jonathan Cape, 1962.

London Topographical Records, Office of the London Topographical Society.

MacKenzie, Gordon *Marylebone—Great City North of Oxford Street.* MacMillan & Co., 1972.

Mayhew, Henry *London Labour and London Poor.* 1851.

Medford, Humphrey *Early Victorian England*, Vol I, 1830–65. Oxford University Press, 1934.

Mee, Arthur *The King's England, London: The City and Westminster.* Hodder and Stoughton, 1937.

Names of Streets and Places. London County Council, 1912, 1929, 1955–56.

Olsen, Donald J. *The Growth of Victorian London.* Batsford, 1976.

Olsen, Donald J. *Town Planning in London—The 18th and 19th Centuries.* Yale University Press, 1964.

Planning News. Jan./Feb. 1980. Royal Borough of Kensington and Chelsea.

Post Office Directories. Kelly & Co.

Riches, Anne 'London Mews Arches', *Architectural Review*, April 1972.

Riches, Anne 'A Survey of Mews Arches In the Royal Borough of Kensington and Chelsea', unpublished 1972.

Shepard, Ernest H. *Drawn From Memory.* Methuen, 1957.

Sheppard, F. H. W. (Ed) *Surveys of London.* Volumes 37, 38, 39. Greater London Council.

'Three London Estates' *The Journal of the London Society.* No. 371, July 1965, pp. 27–28.

Timbs, John *Curiosities of London—Rare and Remarkable Objects of Interest In The Metropolis*, second ed. John Camden Hotten, 1867.

Toplis, Gordon 'Back-to-Front Splendour in Bayswater: The History of Tyburnia II' *Country Life*, November 22, 1973, pp. 1708–1710.

Toplis, Gordon 'Urban Classicism in Decline: The History of Tyburnia I' *Country Life*, November 15, 1973, pp. 1526–1528.

Wheatley, H. B. and Cunningham *London Past and Present.* Volumes 1, 2, 3. J. Murray, 1891.

Acknowledgements

Much of our information was drawn from the following sources: Gillian Bebbington's extensive survey *London Street Names*; Donald J. Olsen's important works *Town Planning in London in the 18th and 19th Centuries* and *The Growth of Victorian London*; the unpublished study *A Survey of Mews Arches* by GLC historian Anne Riches; the *Survey of London* series, now edited by Professor F. H. W. Sheppard, which has been invaluable in our research.

The quotation on pages 24 and 26 is from Frank E. Huggett's *Carriages at Eight*, Lutterworth Press, 1979, p. 39.

The quotation on page 27 is from 'Seventy Years Back', which was published in the *Architectural Review*, December 1958.

We are grateful to the Bedford Estate Office and the staffs of the well-organized local history libraries, particularly Kensington, Marylebone and Victoria, and we also wish to thank the staffs of the British Library, the Guildhall Library and the RIBA Library, as well as those of the history library, photographic and map collection, and the historic buildings division, of the Greater London Council. At all of the above we were able to obtain photographs and to gather much information on the history of estates, and consult documents, leases, rent and rate books, maps and directories. We are also extremely grateful to Victor Belcher, assistant editor of the *Survey of London*, for reading the manuscript and offering many valuable suggestions.

Illustrations
The authors and publishers also acknowledge the following suppliers of copyright photographs:

Godfrey New Photographics Ltd 94, 97; Greater London Council 33, 46 (left), 63, 81 (top), 83, 118 (top left), 139; Guildhall Library 18; Royal Borough of Kensington & Chelsea and Robert Martin Associates 135 (above left); Royal Borough of Kensington & Chelsea Libraries and Arts Service 52, 64 (above), 70, 71, 77; Survey of London 16, 20 (below), 21, 67, 119 (above right); Trustees of the Bedford Estate 8–9, 20 (above), 25 (above and below), 28, 132; Westminster City Libraries 14–15, 34, 36, 40 (below), 49 (left), 112 (above and below).

All other photographs were specially taken by Christopher Wormald.

Index

Numbers in italics refer to illustrations